MAQUISTA CHAPADO

MAQUISTA CHAPADO

Vocabulary and Expressions in Macao's Portuguese Creole

Miguel Senna Fernandes and Alan Norman Baxter

Translated by Marie Imelda MacLeod

Macao 2004

Instituto Cultural do Governo da Região Especial Administrativa de Macau
Avenida de Amizade, Praceta de Miramar, No. 87-U, Edifício San On, Macao

Printed in the Macao Special Administrative Region, People's Republic of China

ISBN 99937-0-069-X

INDEX

INTRODUCTION

1. The purpose of this vocabulary

The compilation of a lexicon of the Portuguese lexically-based Creole of Macao, the Maquista language, has always been a challenge for all of those who have studied this language. Lured by its richness of expression and its fascinating history, few can resist the temptation to research the meanings and origins of its words. A particular attraction lies in the fact that this language mirrors a community which has always chosen a unique way of being, in terms of social and cultural coexistence, in the unique context of Macao.

Over the years, from Marques Pereira (1984 [1899/1901]), Dalgado (1982 [1919]), Santos Ferreira (1996, 1967), through to Batalha (1988 [1977]), and several others, various lists of Maquista Creole words and expressions have been compiled. These compilations have several sources: either as part of research discussions, or as simple vocabulary lists annexed to other works relating to Maquista, or as entire research glossaries. However, most of these earlier studies are not readily accessible to the general public.

The present volume is not a substitute for these previous works. Neither does it aspire to be the last word on this Creole. First and foremost, it aims at providing a unified lexical reference of Maquista. Secondly, it gives an updated, unified presentation of the scattered existing vocabulary, listing words that, although not included in the old Creole texts, are accepted as an integral part of the dialect in its most genuine form (the term for this genuineness being *chapado*) Finally, the work incorporates other, more modern, Macanese expressions, which have a specific meaning in the context of Macau.

The Portuguese lexically-based Creole language of Macao (Baxter 1996, Holm 1989) has been referred to by several names, including *Língu Nhonha*, *Papiâ Cristâm di Macau, Papiaçâm, Patuá, Maquista.* However, while not wanting to discuss the respective merits of these designations, we believe that the term Maquista or Macaísta (generally pronounced [ma'kista]) allows for a wider scope when referring to the linguistic reality. In fact, whereas the term *Patuá* refers to the most archaic, and perhaps more Creole form of the dialect, the term Maquista goes beyond it and permits more flexibility from a linguistic perspective. Thus, Maquista encompasses the whole spectrum of registers of the Macanese language, from the oldest to the most modern, and thus meets our goals. Furthermore, *maquista* means exactly that which pertains to the Macanese.

This vocabulary is conceived as a practical tool of reference, both for those who are acquainted with Maquista, and those who have no previous knowledge of this language. Thus, each main entry is followed by a phonetic transcription and a grammatical classification, which will be explained below. However, in contrast with Batalha's work (1988), the current vocabulary has no pretence of being complete, and it is not encyclopaedic. The reader who wishes to study the language in depth should consult the references provided at the end of this chapter.

2. Organization criteria

We have adopted several criteria in the selection of entries. In most cases, the Maquista words and expressions listed here consist of (i) forms provided by individuals consulted in Macao, Hong Kong, Portugal, the United States of America, and Canada; (ii) forms registered by Batalha (1988) and by Ferreira (1996); and (iii) forms found in the *maquista* literature (Pereira 1984, Barreiros 1942), or in other works on *maquista* culture (Silva 1999, Lamas 1997). While incorporating items defined already by Batalha or Ferreira, it was decided to maintain the minimal definitions supplied by these authors as far as possible. However, at the same time, some of the definitions from those basic works were revised so as to make them clearer.

When consulting the sources listed below, an attempt was made to include only those words and expressions whose meaning was clear in the original context and whose grammatical class could be readily defined. Nevertheless, in contrast with Batalha (1988), no attempt was made to classify the entries as "current" or "formerly used".

From the ouset of the preparation of the vocabulary, it was necessary to take into account the phenomenon of decreolization (i.e., in simple terms, the continuous influence of the Portuguese language on the grammar, phonology and lexicon of Maquista) as well as the continuous influence of Cantonese and English. Due to constant contact with the Portuguese language it is possible to say that even the more conservative speakers of Maquista would have also used words from modern or current Portuguese. In fact, when one considers the fact that the Maquista and Portuguese languages were always in mutual contact, in one way or the other, it may be said that the mixing of words from Portuguese, Cantonese and, to a lesser extent English, was always part of Maquista discourse. This process is at the root of the origins of Maquista.

The present volume avoids the unnecessary duplication resulting from the inclusion of words and expressions from modern Portuguese, Cantonese, or English, which do not show any degree of assimilation to the Maquista system in terms of pronunciation, grammatical function, or semantics. Thus, the vocabulary presented here includes only those words that exhibit some degree of assimilation to the Maquista system and are different in meaning, grammatical function or pronunciation from their Portuguese, English or Cantonese counterparts.

3. Structure of the entries

The following examples show the typical structure of the entries in the vocabulary:

> **Chubí** [ču'bi] *vt* (<*M. cubit*)
> 1. To pinch. *Qui-foi chubí iou?* Why are you pinching me? *Já chubí braço* he pinched my arm.
> 2. To break off a piece of bread, cake or to pick off the petals of a flower. *Chubí pâm* to break bread into pieces.

The entry begins with the main word **Chubí**, followed by a phonetic representation of the pronunciation [ču'bi], and a grammatical definition ***vt*** (transitive verb). Whenever possible, the entry may also indicate the etymology of the main entry in the case of words which do not derive from Portuguese. Therefore, in the above example, the etymology of the word is shown as *(<M. cubit)*, indicating that the word derives from

Malay *cubit.* Then, the definition of the word follows. If the main entry has more than one meaning, the several meanings will be numbered. In this case, in the above example, the word **chụbí** has two basic meanings: "1. To pinch" and "2. To break off a piece of bread, etc". The entries in this vocabulary may also include examples and expressions related to the main entry. Such examples are shown in bold italics, indented after each main definition, as in the above example.

In many entries, in addition to the examples of thc usual use of the main entry, examples of additional expressions based on the main entry are included in bold italics followed by the phonetic transcription. The following is an example with that format:

> **Torâ** [tǫ'rạ] *vt*
>
> To toast. *Torâ pâm* to toast bread.
>
> ***Torâ português*** [tǫ'rạ portu'gẹs] used to describe a person who can speak perfect Portuguese, with an affected accent.

In certain instances, among the examples of expressions related to the main entry there are expressions preceded by the symbol v. These are expressions which do not have already any direct semantic connection with the meaning of the main entry.

Finally, in some other instances, a given term may display more than one pronunciation and/or more than one spelling. In such cases, each variant is included in an independent entry that refers to the main entry where the definition of the word is located. However, this work does not attempt to rigorously list all the orthographic variants found in Maquista literature.

4. The orthography of Maquista

The orthography of standard Portuguese is in many ways inadequate for representing the pronunciation of Maquista. This is so because Maquista contains various sounds which do not exist in Portuguese and which, therefore, are incapable of being represented by that alphabet. Thus, the underlined section of the Maquista word **chubí** is pronounced as **ch** in English or Spanish, which is represented by [č] in phonetic transcription[1] It is not pronounced like the Portuguese **ch** which is similar to **sh** in English, which is represented by [š] in phonetic transcription.

Another problem arises with the Maquista words that derive from Portuguese words containing nasal vowels. Let us consider, for instance, the word **nação** (nation). In Portuguese, this word is pronounced with a nasal diphthong [nasãũ)], whereas in Maquista the equivalent word is pronounced with a vowel (generally non-nasal) followed by a nasal consonant [na'saŋ]. Here, the symbol [ŋ] represents a sound that occurs in word final position in many languages, as in the English **sing** [siŋ]. However, the sound [ŋ] does not occur in word final position in Portuguese.

The problem may be summed up in the following way: most words in Maquista are derived from Portuguese words, however total phonetic correspondence occurs only in a few cases. In the great majority of cases, the pronunciation of Maquista words is different from that of the Portuguese. In these cases, if we were to write Maquista words using the Standard Portuguese orthography for the equivalent word, we would

[1] [č], a palatal unvoiced affricate consonant.

convey the absolutely wrong impression that such words share the same pronunciation in Maquista and Portuguese!

From the perspective of linguistic science, the ideal solution for such problems is the creation of an orthography that accurately represents the sounds of Maquista. Such an initiative was undertaken in recent years in the case of the Portuguese lexically-based Creole languages of Cape Verde (Quint 2000), Guinea-Bissau (Scantamburlo 1999), and Malacca (Baxter 1988, Baxter & de Silva, 2004). However, in the case of Maquista such an initiative is not suitable for several reasons. First, there is already a considerable body of Maquista literature from the 19th and 20th centuries written in an orthography based on Standard Portuguese, an orthography that was further perfected by Ferreira (1996). In view of the fact that the language today has very few speakers with full natural linguistic competence, this corpus of literature represents an invaluable asset of the Maquista language. Thus, in preparing a reference vocabulary, it is essential to adopt an orthography that guarantees similarity with the traditional orthographies, thereby facilitating access to extant written materials.[2]

The present vocabulary largely follows the orthography proposed by Ferreira (1996), but includes certain changes and standardizations, namely:

[2] The ideal would be to follow the good example of other Portuguese lexically-based Creoles and to formulate a simple and transparent orthography, easy to read and easy to use. The links with the existing orthographies could be kept with the inclusion in a single volume, with cross references, of all traditional orthographies. Unfortunately, this work is beyond the scope of the present vocabulary.

(i) The consonant [ŋ] in syllable final position is represented by **ng'** before a vowel, for example: **ung'a**;
(ii) The consonant [ŋ] in word final position is represented uniformly by **-m**, and the preceding adjacent vowel carries a written accent to indicate that it is not nasal, for example: **pám**, **coraçám**;[3]
(iii)The unstressed vowels /e/ and /o/ in word final position are represented as in the work of Ferreira (1996)[4], but in a more consistent way. The general rule in Maquista regarding these vowels in word final position is the following: the vowel /e/ is pronounced [i] and is generally represented by the letter **i**, and the vowel /o/ is pronounced [u] in some words and [ọ][5] in others, being represented by the letter **o**.

In section **5**, some additional problems relating to the phonetic transcription and orthography are discussed. In section **5.6.** the reader will find a table of examples of correspondences between the orthography used in this vocabulary and the phonetic transcription included in the entries.

---

[3] In reality, the most sensible solution in the case of the consonant [ŋ], both in syllable final position within a word (**ung'a**) and in a word final syllable (**coraçám**), would be to adopt the grapheme **ng** in all cases. Thus, we would have **ung'a** and **coraçáng**.

[4] However, the orthography used by Ferreira (1996) is somewhat inconsistent regarding this matter. In many words ending in unstressed [i], Santos Ferreira uses the letter **i**, for instance **chávi** key, **pónti** bridge, **di** of, **qui** that. Nevertheless, in many other words ending in unstressed [i] such as **chilicote**, the author uses the letter **e** to represent the final vowel. As we said above, the general Maquista rule, as well as in many varieties of Portuguese and in Portuguese lexically-based Creole languages, is that an unstressed **e** in word final position is pronounced as [i]. In view of these facts, the simplest solution is to adopt a single consistent orthographic representation: use the letter **i**.

5. Phonetic transcription

The phonetic transcriptions included in the vocabulary entries are intended as a guide to the pronunciation of Maquista words, because the pronunciation cannot be adequately deduced from the Portuguese-based spelling. Moreover, the inclusion of phonetic transcriptions is essential for those readers who do not know Maquista. Although it is well known that this language displays considerable variation under the influence of Portuguese, the present work adopts a conservative approach. Thus, the phonetic transcription used is consonant with the traditional phonological characteristics of Maquista and represents the pronunciation that Batalha (1988) calls <antígua> (archaic). This was done in an attempt to facilitate the maintenance of the traditional pronunciation of the Creole.

---

[5] This [ọ] is more closed than its Modern European Portuguese counterpart and is phonologically equivalent to unstressed [u]. These facts regarding the unstressed vowels /e/ and /o/ in word final position resemble the situations found in varieties of overseas Portuguese, such as the former archaic varieties of Portuguese spoken in Timor, Goa, Damão, and are also similar to the situation on Brazilian Portuguese in general. All of these varieties of Portuguese are historically based on the pronunciation of 18th century (or even older) Portuguese. In all these overseas varieties of Portuguese word final unstressed /e/ and /o/ are pronounced as /i/ and /u/, respectively. This is also the situation in other varieties of Portuguese Creole (in Cape Verde, Guinea-Bissau, São Tomé, Príncipe, Annobón (Anobom in Portuguese), Daman, Korlai, and Malacca). In the case of Maquista, to judge by the indecision of Ferreira (1996) in representing unstressed **o** in word final position, it is very likely that in former times the pronunciation of this vowel was [u]. In modern times, as the language has been progressively losing its native speakers, while undergoing strong pressure from written and spoken metropolitan Portuguese, the medium high stressed back vowel [o] has changed towards unstressed Portuguese [ọ] in word end position.

The phonetic transcriptions are given in a broad phonetic notation which captures the salient characteristics of Maquista pronunciation.[6] The reason for using broad phonetic transcription rather than narrow transcription is that the latter would require an acoustic analysis of the recordings of several Maquista speakers pronouncing every single word and expression in the vocabulary. Only then would a narrow phonetic transcription be possible. Without a complete acoustic analysis of the Maquista sounds, it is impossible and highly imprudent to elaborate on details of its phonological system, as there is a real risk of making assertions that are not empirically justified.

5.1. Vowels

Maquista vowels, with rare exceptions due to the influence of modern Portuguese pronunciation, show minimal reduction in unstressed syllables and little differentiation of openness and closure. Moreover, in comparison to Portuguese, the vowels /a/, /e/ and /o/ in Maquista, when stressed, are considerably unstable in terms of openness. We thus agree with Batalha (1988:16), that the quality of /a/, /e/ and /o/ varies considerably from speaker to speaker, so much so that in many cases it is impossible to attribute consistent specifications to these three vowels.

Batalha began her research in the 1950s, working closely with native speakers of Maquista at a time when there were still a fair number of

[6] In this sense, except in some more obvious cases, we do not indicate phonological assimilation phenomena between words, for the simple reason that it would require consideration of data from an acoustic analysis.

fully fluent speakers. It is fair to assume that her phonetic representations accurately represent earlier stages of Maquista. Generally speaking, there are no major differences between our transcriptions and those of Batalha. However, with respect to one important aspect of Maquista phonology, we diverge from the transcriptions presented in Batalha, i.e., in the transcription of nasal segments (see Batalha 1988:16). This will be explained in detail in the following section.

5.2. Consonants: nasal segments

In contrast with the transcription used by Batalha (1988:16), where the syllable final nasal consonants are represented by placing the symbol (~) over a vowel or by **-m**[7], we transcribe these nasal segments as full consonants. Considering the recordings of Maquista speakers of the last 40 years, and in consultation with Prof. Emeritus R. W. Thompson, of La Trobe University, who conducted research on Maquista in the 1950s and 1960s, and in consultation with Prof. Jean-Michel Charpentier, who recorded and analysed the Maquista of elderly speakers in Hong Kong and Macao, in the 1980s, we came to the conclusion that the Maquista phonological system does not contain nasal vowels, although they may appear variably due to the decreolization process. Therefore, where the Portuguese pronunciation of the word **tem** is [tẽ], the pronunciation of the equivalent Maquista word would be [teŋ]. Similarly, the pronunciation of the Portuguese

[7] Batalha explains that these two mechanisms are used to represent a nasal consonant in syllable final position. However, we consider that the use of (~) conveys the wrong impression that the nasalization of vowels was a characteristic of early Maquista.

word **nação** is [nasãũ], while the traditional pronunciation of the equivalent word in Maquista would be [na'sáŋ]. In sum, where Portuguese has nasal vowels and nasal diphthongs, Maquista has only oral vowels and sequences of oral vowel + nasal consonant. This reality is reflected in the phonetic transcription used in this vocabulary as well as in the orthography.

5.3. Main syllable stress and the written accents used in the orthography of this vocabulary

Most Maquista words have a stressed penultimate syllable, as in Portuguese. Exceptions to this rule are indicated by a written accent. To this effect, the (^) and (´) accents are used. In the present work these written accents have the following values:

The circumflex accent (^) indicates a closed stressed **e**, **a** or **o** vowel, in any position in the word:

ôlo	[‘ọlu]	eye
abolô	[abo’lọ]	lacquered box
comê	[kọ’mẹ]	eat
bêzo	[‘bẹzu]	kiss
falâ	[fạ’lạ]	speak
pônto	[‘pọntu]	bridge
sâm	[sạŋ]	being

The acute accent (´) indicates the principal stressed syllable in the following cases:

(i) on the vowels **e**, **a**, and **o**, it indicates a (semi-) open vowel,[8] for instance:

mulé	[mu'lẹ]	woman, wife
nuncassá	[nuŋka's**a**]	it is not needed
corasám	[kọra's**a**ŋ][9]	heart

(ii) on stressed **i** and **u** vowels in word final position, for instance:

izizí	[izi'zi]	to demand

<u>Both the circumflex accent (^)</u> and the acute accent (´), when placed on a vowel that is followed by a nasal consonant, besides indicating the tonic syllable of polysyllables, and the degree of openness of the vowel, have the additional function of indicating that the vowel is not nasalized:

vêm	[vẹŋ]	to come
pám	[pạŋ]	bread
coraçám	[kọra'saŋ]	heart

5.4. The phonetic representation of compounds and phrasal expressions

During the preparation of this vocabulary, we noticed that, in composites and in phrasal lexical expressions, there are alterations in the main stress on a word according to the speed of the utterance. The general trend in

[8] However, as discussed in section 5.1., the openness of these vowels varies considerably in degree.

[9] Except in **sâm** 'ser' (be). In most words that end in **-am**, the /a/ vowel varies in quality between semi-open and open.

these cases is for the last main stress in a sequence of words to be the strongest while the main stresses on the previous words become secondary or are neutralized. In order to avoid complicating the phonetic transcription, and also because this phenomenon appears to depend on an intonation rule governed by the speed of the utterance, except in a few conspicuous cases, we have transcribed each word as a unit with its own stress weight.

5.5. The hyphen

The hyphen is used in the following cases:

(i) in reduplications, for instance: **filo-filo** children/sons;
(ii) in compounds, for instance: **abela-mestra** "know-all";
(iii) between a noun or pronoun and a following genitive particle, for instance: **êle-sa casa** his house, **iou-sa filo** my son, **Pedro-sa mulé** Pedro's wife;
(iv) between an expletive adverb and the focalized element, for instance **vêm-ia** come!

5.6. Orthographic and phonetic correspondences

The following table lists the letters and the corresponding phonetic symbols that are used:

Letter	Phonetic symbol	Example
p	[p]	**perdê** to lose
b	[b]	**babo** saliva
t	[t]	**tambâ** to patch

d	[d]		**dâle** to hit
f	[f]		**filo** son
v	[v]		**vêm** to come
s	[s]		**sai** to go out
ç	[s]		**papiaçám** "speech"
ss	[s]		**assí** thus
z	[z]		**zuní** to buzz
l	[l]		**letrado** lawyer
r	[r]		**riva** up, as verb
m	[m]		**mai** mother
n	[ɱ]		**enfadâ** to bore
n	[n]		**na** in/on
-m	[ŋ]		**naçám** nation
ng'	[ŋ]		**ung'a** one
nh	[ɲ]		**nhame** yam
lh	[λ]		**falhâ** fail
ch	[č]		**chuva** rain
j	[ǰ]		**justo** fair
c	[k]		**cási** almost
c	[s]	before **e** or **i**	**mercê** thanks
i	[y]	stressed vowel /i/ before **a** or **o**	**iou** me, **laia** kind, thing
i	[i]		**izizí** to demand
-e	[i]	/i/ vowel	**bagate** spell
-i	[i]	/i/ vowel	**úndi** where
e	[ę]	open stressed /e/ vowel	**gréza** church
é	[ę]	open stressed /e/ vowel	**mulé** woman
e	[ę]	open unstressed /e/ vowel	**dessâ** to leave
ê	[ẹ]	closed stressed /e/ vowel	**pêsse** fish

e	[ẹ]	closed unstressed /e/ vowel	**bezâ** to kiss
e	[e]	mid unstressed /e/	**ezazerâ** to exagerate
á	[ą]	open stressed /a/	**babá** boy
a	[a]	mid stressed /a/ vowel	**ade** duck
a	[a]	mid unstressed /a/ vowel	**fumiga** ant
â	[ạ]	closed stressed /a/ vowel	**falâ** to speak
o	[o]	mid unstressed /o/ vowel	**corenteza** current
ó	[ǫ]	open stressed /a/ vowel	**pónti** bridge
o	[ǫ]	open unstressed /o/ vowel	**pontâ** to point
ô	[ọ]	closed stressed /o/ vowel	**ôlu** eye
o	[ọ]	closed unstressed /o/ vowel	**bolo** cake
u	[u]	stressed /u/ vowel	**ung'a** one
u	[u]	unstressed /u/ vowel	**mulé** woman
u	[w]	/u/ before **a** or **o**	**aguado** liquified
u	[w]	in syllable final position	**mau** bad, evil
h	no phonetic value (i.e., not pronounced)		**hoze** today
h	[h]	in some words derived from Cantonese	**hám-chói** salted preserved vegetables.

The main stress in phonetic transcriptions is indicated by the symbol <‘>, placed before the stressed syllable, for instance [‘čuva] ‘chuva’ (rain).

6. Grammatical representation

Each main entry is followed by a grammatical definition based on the function of the word in the Maquista grammar. It is important to stress that the grammatical functions of words in Maquista may be totally different from those of Portuguese. We recommend readers who are interested in the grammatical structure of Maquista to consult the grammatical sketch by Ferreira (1996:229-251), and also the studies by Charpentier (1992) and Thompson (1959, 1960).

6.1. Acronyms of grammatical and lexicographic terminology

The following acronyms are used in this text:

adj	adjective
adv	adverb
aff	affirmation
comp	compound
conj	conjunction
dem	demonstrative
det	determiner
euph	euphemism
subst. exp.	nominalized expression
fem	feminine
Fig	figurative
interj	interjection
interrog	interrogative
Lit	literally
masc	masculine
n	noun

neg	negator
part	particle
prep	preposition
pej	pejorative
pro	pronoun
quant	quantifier
rel	relative pronoun
syn	synonym
t.m.a part.	tense, mood or aspect particle
t.m.a part. neg.	negative tense, mood or aspect particle
f.a.	term of address
cop.v.	copular verb
vi	intransitive verb
m.v.	modal verb
vt	transitive verb

7. Etymology

The Maquista language, as any other language with origins in a multilingual context, has in its lexicon words from several sources, which have undergone different influences and developments. In this sense, most Maquista words are of Portuguese origin, but diverge from that source in that they have pronunciations, grammatical functions or meanings that are peculiar to Maquista. At the same time, Maquista contains words of non-Portuguese origins, which were assimilated into the Maquista system over the years. In order of greater to lesser influence, the contribution of non-Portuguese languages is: Malay and Cantonese[10], English, Koncanin-Marata, Japonese, Tamil-Malaialam, Sanskrit, Persian, Arabic, Hindustani, Dutch, Spanish[11] , French and Dravidian. The etymological acronyms used are:

C.	Cantonese
D.	Dutch
Dr.	Dravidian
E.	English
Fr.	French
Hin.	Hindustani
I-P.	Indo-Portuguese
J.	Japanese
Kon.	Koncanin
M.	Malay
Mal.	Malaialam
Maq.	Maquista[12]
P.	Portuguese
Per.	Persian
Sanskr.	Sanskrit
Sp.	Spanish
T.	Tamil

[10] The nine tones of Cantonese are shown in the etymologies by means of a number system. In the majority of cases, the corresponding Chinese characters are also included. In some cases, it was not possible to provide characters, for the simple reason that the words in question were of a colloquial nature and, hence, unwritten.

[11] There is a popular belief that the word **adiós** (goodbye) in Maquista has a Spanish origin. However, the source of the word is as Portuguese as is that of the word **iou (I)**. The explanation for the phonological divergence stems from two factors: (i) regional Portuguese pronunciations wherein the segment /e/ of the diphthong /eu/ is more closed than in metropolitan Portuguese; and (ii) the interface between the phonology of Portuguese and the phonologies of Asian languages such as Malay and Cantonese, among others. Other words, such as **bisagra** (door or window hinge), listed by Batalha (1988:320) as being of Spanish origin, may equally be of regional Portuguese origin. However, there are certain words registered in this vocabulary as genuinely Spanish and these may stem from two historical sources. Some, as for instance **chiste** 'natural grace', may have arrived via regional forms of the Portuguese language, that were in contact with Spanish. Others, as for example, **assafata** 'female servant', may have arrived from the Phillipines.

[12] Used in some Maquista word derivations.

Bibliographic references

Barreiros, Danilo Leopoldo. 1943/44. 'O dialecto português de Macau'. Special issue of *Renascimento*, Macao, 1943-1944.

Batalha, Graciete Nogueira. 1988 [1977]. *Glossário do Dialecto Macaense - Notas linguísticas, etnográficas e folclóricas*. Macao: Instituto Cultural de Macau.

Baxter, Alan N. 1988. *A Grammar of Kristang (Malacca Creole Portuguese).* Canberra: Pacific Linguistics.

Baxter, Alan N. 1996. 'Portuguese and Creole Portuguese in the Pacific and Western Pacific rim'. In Stephen A. Wurm, Peter Mühlhäusler & Darrell T. Tryon (eds.) *Atlas of Languages of Intercultural Communication in the Pacific, Asia and the Americas*, pp.301-338.

Baxter, Alan N. & de Silva, Patrick. [2004.] *A Dictionary of Kristang (Malacca Creole Portuguese).* Canberra: Pacific Linguistics.

Charpentier, Jean-Michel. 1992. 'La survivance du créole portugais 'Makaísta' en Extrême-Orient'. In Ernesto d'Andrade & Alain Kihm (eds.) *Actas do Colóquio sobre 'Crioulos de Base Lexical Portuguesa'*, pp.81-96. Lisboa: Colibri.

Dalgado, Sebastião Rodolfo. 1982. *Glossário Luso-Asiático.* Hamburg: Helmut Buske Verlag. [Reprint of the 1919 edition.]

Ferreira, José dos Santos. 1996. *Papiaçám di Macau.* Macao: Fundação Macau.

Ferreira, José dos Santos. 1967. *Macau sã assi.* Macao: Tipografia da Missão do Padroado.

Forjaz, Jorge 1996, *Famílias Macaenses (3 Vols.).* Macao: Fundação Oriente.

Holm, John. 1989. *Pidgins and Creoles. Volume II Reference Survey.* Cambridge: Cambridge University Press.

Lamas, João António Ferreira. 1997. *A Culinária dos Macaenses*. Porto: Lello Editores.

Pereira, José Feliciano Marques. 1984 (reprint of articles compiled in 1899-1901) "Subsídios para o estudo dos dialectos crioulos do Extremo Oriente" in *TA-SSI-YANG-KUO – Arquivo e Anais do Extremo Oriente Português*, Série I. Macao: Arquivo Histórico de Macau.

Quint, Nicolas. 2000. *Grammaire de la Langue Cap-Verdienne.* Paris: L'Harmattan.

Reinecke, John E., DeCamp, David., Hancock, Ian F., Tsuzaki, Stanley M., & Wood, Richard E. 1975. *A Bibliography of Pidgin and Creole Languages.* Honolulu: The University of Hawaii Press.

Scatamburlo, Luigi. 1999. *Dicionário do Guineense. Vol 1. Introdução e notas gramaticais.* Lisboa: Colibri.

Silva, Frederic A. 1999. *Things I Remember.* San Francisco: [Author's edition].

Tomás, Maria Isabel. 1992. *Os Crioulos Portugueses do Oriente. Uma bibliografia.* Macao: Instituto Cultural de Macau.

Thompson, Robert Wallace. 1959. 'Two synchronic cross-sections of the Portuguese dialect of Macao'. *Orbis* 8:29-53.

Thompson, Robert Wallace. 1950. 'O dialecto português de Hong Kong'. *Boletim de Filologia* (Lisboa) 19:289-293.

VOCABULARY

Abacate [aba'kạti] *n*
Avocado (*Persea gratissima*).

Abâno [a'bạnu] See **Avano**.

Abêla-mestra [a'bela 'mestra] *n*
Know-all, woman who thinks she knows everything.

Ablô [a'blọ] See **Abolô**.

Abolô [abo'lọ], **ablô** [a'blọ], **abulô** [abu'lọ] *n* (<*C. hap⁹ lo¹* 合蘿)
1. Traditional lacquered box for keeping cakes, biscuits and sweets.
2. Round basket with lid and handles.

Abulô [abu'lọ] See **Abolô**.

Abusadéra [abuza'dẹra] See **abusadôr**.

Abusadôr [abuza'dọ] *adj & n masc* **abusadéra** [abuza'déra] *adj & n fem*
Daring, cheeky, insolent, arrogant.

Abuta [a'butạ] *n*
Plant in the *Menispermaceae* family, formerly used in Macao for preparing ***mezinha três pau***.

Achâ [a'čạ] *vt*
1. To find.
2. To discover, find out.
3. To receive.

Ach'á [ač'a] *n* (<*C. a³ tsa¹* 阿差)
Moor, Indian Muslim.

Achaque [a'čaki] *n*
Common ailment. *Achaque di cabeça* headache. *Achaque di romatismo* rheumatic pains. *Achaque di idade* old age complaints.

Achar [a'ča] *n*
Vegetable or fruit preserve, made of spring onions, cabbage, coconut, apple, pear, etc. , in vinegar and salt.

Achi-môco [a'či 'mọku] *n* (<*C. a³ tsi¹* 阿痴)
Idiot, fool.

Acung'a [a' kuŋa] *dem.*
That. *Acung'a quanto* those.

Adáp [a'dap] *adj* (<*Eng. hard up*)
Hard-up, broke.

Ade ['adi] *n*
Duck. *Ade salgado s*alted duck in brine. *Ade-cabidela* duck stew with duck's blood.
Voz di ade-macho [vọs di 'adi 'maču] duck's voice, hoarse or husky voice.
See **Bafo, *Báfo di ade***.

Adiós [adi'ọs] *adv*
Goodbye.
Adiós minha vôs! [adi'ọs 'miŋa vọs] Expression of impatience, irritation. *Mau Maria, adiós minha vôs!* get lost!

A-Fat [a'fat] *n* (<*C. a*[3] *fad*[8] 阿發)
Fool, gauche. *Cara di a-fat* stupid-looking. *Jêto di a-fat* vulgar.

Afét [a'fet] *adj & n* (<*Eng. fat*)
Fatty, a chubby person.

Afiâ [afi'ạ] *vt*
To sharpen.

Afiám [a'fyaŋ] *n*
Opium.

Afinâ [afi'nạ] *vt*
1. To tune, put in the right tone.
2. To make someone angry. *Nê-bôm afinâ iou* don't make me angry. *Êle já ficâ quelê afinado* he became very angry.

Afinado [afi'nạdọ] *adj*
1. In tune.
2. Angry. *Êle já ficâ quelê afinado* he became very angry.

Afogosa [afo'gosa] See **Afogoso**.

Afogoso [afo'gọso] *adj masc,* **afogosa** [afo'gosa] *adj fem*
Hurried, impetuous, inconsiderate. *Nê-bôm assí afogoso* don't be so impetuous.

Afordâ [afọr'dạ] *vt* (<*Eng. afford*)

To provide, support, have the means to.

Afugâ [afu'gạ] *vi & vt*
1. To drown.
2. To suffocate, asfixiate.

Agar-agar [a'gar a'gar] *n* (<*M. agar-agar*)
Algae used to make jelly.

Agradada [agra'dạda] See **agradado.**

Agradado [agra'dạdu] *adj masc*, **agradada** [agra'dạda] *adj fem*
1. Nice.
2. Pleasant.

Água ['agu] *n*
Water. *Água pa banhâ* bathwater.
Ágú-bento ['agu 'bẹntu] holy water.
Ágú-chêro ['agu 'čẹru] perfume.
Ágú-dóci ['agu 'dọsi] or ***ágú-fonti*** ['agu 'fọnti] drinking water.

Aguâ [a'gwạ] *vi*
1. To fly. *Pastro tâ aguâ* the bird is flying.
2. To run fast. *Aguâ vai riva* to climb up very quickly.

Aguadêra [agwa'dẹra] *n*
Water carrier, woman who carries water drawn from wells and fountains.

Aguado [a'gwadu] *adj*
1. Diluted, mixed with water.
2. Liquified.

Aguchám [agu'čaŋ] *n* (<*Maq. agu* + <*C. ha[1] tsang[1]* 蝦繒)
Small, portable fishing net, for use by one person. See **Sarambau**.

Aia! [ại'ạ] *interj*
Interjection expressing fear, surprise, pain, impatience. *Aia! Qui boniteza* how beautiful! *Aia, qui susto!* how frightening!

Alí [a'li] *adv*
There. *Ali-riva,* up there. *Ali-vánda,* over there.

Alo [‘alu] See **Alio**.

Álio [‘aliu], **alo** [‘alu] *n*
Garlic.
Álio co cobra [‘aliu ko ‘kǫbra] sworn enemies.

Alicrim [ali’kriŋ] *n*
Rosemary (*Rosmarinus officinalis*).

Algudám [algu’daŋ] *n*
Cotton. See **Panha**.

Algudêro [algu’dẹro] See Á**rve di panha**.

Almis [al’mis] *adj*
Musky. See **Amiz**.

Alonço [a’lǫnsu] *n*
Idiot, person who does not listen or hear.
Finzí alonço [fin’zi a’lǫnsu] to play the fool, pretend not to hear.

Alúa [a’lua], **aluá** [alu’a] *n*
Traditional Macanese Christmas sweetmeat.

Aluá [alu’a] See **Alúa**.

Alucinado [alusi’nadu] *adj*
Out of one’s mind, confused.

Alumiâ [alu’miạ] See **Lumiâ**.

Ama [‘ama] *n*
Maid, domestic servant. Woman paid to carry out domestic duties.
Ama-lete [‘ama ’lẹti] wet nurse.
Ama-seco [‘ama ’sẹku] nursery nurse.

Amascâ [amas’kạ] *vi*
To work as a domestic servant, work hard.

Ambâ [am’bạ], **ambâc** [am’bạk], **hambâc** [ham’bạk] *vt* (<*Eng? humbug*, <*M? hamba, hambat, hambek*).
To take advantage of somebody else’s weakness, innocence or good faith. *Vôs nê-bôm ambâ ela!* don’t take advantage of her, don’t intimidate her!

Ambâc [am'bạk] See **Ambâ**.

Amechóm [am'čọŋ] *n* (<*C. am*[7] *tsong*[1] *掩盅*)
Rough clay pot glazed on the inside, for storing home-made preserves.

Amen [a'meŋ] *interj*
Yes, consent, agreement.
Amen-amen [a'meŋ a'meŋ] yes-man.
❖***Amen Jesus*** [a'meŋ ǰe'zus] person with no will of his own, always in agreement.

Amestê [ames'tẹ], **mestê** [mes'tẹ] *v*
It is necessary. See also **Nomestê**.

Amiz [a'mis] *adj* (<*M. hamiz*)
Spoiled, rotten. *Pêsse amiz* rotten fish. *Cherâ amiz* it stinks to high heaven. See **almis**.

Amóque [a'mọk] *adj* (<*M. amok*)
Obsessed with an idea, passion, the extent of foolishness. *Ficâ amóque* he went out of his mind.

Amochâi [amo'cại] *n* (<*P. amor* + *C. chai*[2] *仔*)
Sweety, dear, darling.

Amôr[1] [a'mọ] *adj*
Lovely, quiet, pretty. *Êle qui amôr!* what a lovely child.

Amôr[2] [a'mọ] *n*
Love.

Ampás [am'pas] *n* (<*M. hampas*)
Residue, part of any food, especially fruit and vegetables, that has no nutritional value or cannot be used.
❖***Ampás sim sumo*** [am'pas siŋ'sumu] dull, humourless person.

Amui [a'mui] *n* (<*C. a*[3] *mui*[2] *阿妹*)
Unmarried Chinese girl from humble background.
Amui baléu [a'mui bạ'lẹu] heavily made-up girl carried on a small platform balanced

on the shoulders of two people during certain Chinese ceremonies.

Amuichai [amui'čại] *n* (<*C. a^3 mui^1 tsai^2 阿妹仔*)
Very young Chinese girl or servant. *Amuichai di compra som* servant in charge of market shopping.

Amuiróna [amui'rọna] *n* (<*C. a^3 mui^1 阿妹+ P. -rona*)
Young, well-developed girl.

Ancusa [aŋ'kuza] *n*
1.Thing.
2.Something. *Seléa ancusa* something like this. *Estung'a ancusa* this.

Andâ [an'dạ] *vi*
1. To walk.
2. To go for a walk.
❖***Andâ a nóvi*** [an'dạ a'nọvi] to be busy, be on the go all day.

Anidiu [ani'diu] *n* (<*Eng. honey dew*)
Honey dew melon.

Ano ['anu] *n*
Year.
Ano passado ['anu pa'sadu] last year.
Ano trasado ['anu tra'zadu] two years ago.
Abrí ano [a'bri 'anu] to bring in the New Year (*See. C. h'ói^1 nin^4 開年*).
Fichâ ano [fi'čạ 'anu] to come to the end of the year, have a birthday.

Anona [a'nona] *n*
Custard-apple (*Annona reticulata*) or soursop (*Annona muricata*).

Anôte^1 [a'nọti], **nôte** ['nọti] *adv*
At night. *Anote-anote* in the middle of the night.

Anôte^2 [a'nọti], **nôte** ['nọti] *n*
Night. *Anote-anote* nights.

Ânsia ['aŋsia] *n*
1. Anxiety, ardent desire, pressing concern. *Ansia buscâ* to seek anxiously.

2. Greed, miserliness. *Ânsia feo olâ* it's rude to be greedy.

Antigônço [anti'gonso] *adj*
Old-fashioned.

Antigonôstre [antigo'nọstri] *adj*
Very old. *Casarám antigonôstre* very old mansion.

Apa ['apa] *n* (<*Dr. appam*)
1. Whitish sweet or savoury dumpling made with flour and sticky rice.
Apa-bico ['apa 'biku] savoury crescent-shaped pork dumpling flavoured with spices.
Apa-múchi ['apa 'muči] or ***apa-múchi-coco*** ['apa' mu'či 'koko] sweetmeat made with rice flour.
2. Vulva.
❖***Apa-fêde*** ['apa 'fẹde] promiscuous woman.

Apâi [a'pại] *adj & adv* (<*C. a*[3] *pai*[1] 阿跛)
Lame. *Andâ apai* to limp, hobble.

Apó [a'pọ] *n* (<*C. a*[3] *po*[1] 阿婆)
Elderly Chinese woman of a humble background. *Apó di cartâ águ* woman who carries water.

Apontamento [aponta'mẹntu] *n* (<*Eng. appointment*)
Date, commitment, appointment.

Aporóna [apo'rọna] *n*
Large, heavy, ordinary, middle-aged Chinese woman.

Araviro [ara'viru] See **Arviro**.

Areca [a'reka] *n*
Betel nut. Fruit of the betel nut palm (*Areca catechu*). Very popular amongst Macanese who chewed it with betel leaves. The betel nut is opened with scissors or with a **chilicate**.

Arenga [a'rẹŋga], [a'riŋga] *n*
Scheme.

Arenguéra [ariŋ'gęra] *n*
Schemer, trouble-maker.

Argolinha [argo'liɲa] *n*
Earrings.

Armário-rópa [ar'mariu'rǫpa] *n*
Wardrobe.

Armário-vidro [ar'mariu 'vidru] *n*
Cabinet.

Aronça-aronça [a'rǫnsa 'rǫnsa]
See **Rónça-rónça**.

Arôz [a'rọs] *n*
Rice. *Arôz caregado* rice boiled with salt and shaped in a mould. *Arôz chauchau* fried rice. *Arôz-pulú* sticky rice. *Aroz-gordo* rice stewed with meat.

Arto ['artu] *adj*
Tall.

Artura [ar'tura] *n*
Height.

Aruda [a'ruda] *n*
Rue (*Ruta graveolens*), used for home remedies.

Árve ['arvi] See **Árvre**.

Arvirice [arvi'risi] *n* (<*M. haru biru*)
1. Fun.
2. Naughtiness.
3. Prank.

Arviro[1] [ar'viru], [ari'viru], **araviro** [ara'viru] *adj* (<*M. haru biru*)
Naughty, playful, used to describe somebody who likes to play tricks on others.

Arviro[2] [ar'viru], [ari'viru], **araviro** [ara'viru] *n* (<*M. haru biru*)
1. Trick, prank.
2. Naughty person, somebody who likes to fool around or play pranks.

Árvre ['arvri], **árve** ['arvi] *n*
Tree.
Árve di panha ['arvi di 'paɲa]

silk cotton tree (*Bombax malabaricum*), also called **algudêro**.
Árve S. José [‘arvi sa̤ɲ ǰu’zę] St. Joseph’s (Seminary) tree, weeping fig (*Ficus wightiana*), also called *Árve di gondôm*. See **Gondôm**.
Árve pagode [‘arvi pa’gǫdi] tree such as the banyan fig (*Ficus retusa*).

Asa [‘aza] *n*
1. Wing.
2. Fin.
Asa-di-pêsse [‘aza di ‘pe̤se̤] shark fin.

Asa-amarela [azama’rela] *n*
Seabream, member of the *Sparus* genus common in the Pearl River.

Asinha [a’ziɲa] See **Azinha**.

Asnático [as’naticu] *adj*
Ridiculous, nonsense.

Asnéra [as’nęra] *n*
1. Nonsense, swear word. *Papiâ asneira* to talk nonense.
2. Obscenity. *Asnéra grándi-grándi* Swear word.

Asnerám [asne̤’raŋ] *n*
Man who swears.

Áspro [‘aspru] *adj*
1. Rough.
2. Impolite.

Assafata [asa’fata] *n pej* (<*Sp. azafata*)
Maid.

Assanhâ [asa’ɲa̤] *vt*
1. To provoke.
2. To enrage.

Assanhado [asa’ɲa̤du] *adj*
Furious.

Asséta [a’sęsta] *n*
Siesta. *Durmí assesta* to take a nap.

Assí [a’si] *adv*
1. So, such. *Assí azinha* so fast. *Assí perto* so near. *Quele-*

môdo assí? how's that? *Sâm assí* that's the way it is.
2. Like. *Êle vestí como padre assí* he dresses like a priest. *Saltâ-pulâ como macaco assí* he leaps around like a monkey.
3. Around, approximately. *Quando vôs vêm? Cinco-óra, assi!* when are you coming? At around six.

Assilai [asi'lai] *adv* (<*Maq.* *assí* + *laia*)
1. Similar.
2. Suchlike.
See also **Seléa**.

Astrevê [astre'vẹ] *vi*
To dare. *Iou nádi astrevê* I won't dare.

Astrevido [astre'vidu] *adj*
Daring, disrespectful.

Atachamento [atača'mentu] *n* (<*Eng. attachment*)
Affection, love.

Atâi [a'tại] *n* (<*C. a*[3] *tai*[6] *阿弟*)
1. Chinese boy.
Atâi di rua [a'tại di 'ruạ] uneducated boy.
2. Chinese boy servant.
3. Errand boy.

Atendê [aten'dẹ] *vt* (<*Eng. attend* + *P. atender*)
To be present. *Atendê fonçám* to attend a ceremony.

Atinâ [ati'nạ] *vi*
To get used to. *Nôm pôde atinâ co frio* he can't get used to the cold.

Atirâ [ati'rạ] *vt*
To chuck, throw.
Atirâ di cabeça [ati'rạ di ka'bẹsa] to say, do something without considering the consequences.
❖ ***Atirâ pedra, iscondê mám*** [ati'rạ 'pedra skọn'dẹ maŋ] hypocrite.

Auábe [a'wabi] *n* (<*J. awabi*)
Abalone (*genus Haliotis*).

Auto-china ['awto 'čina] *n*
Chinese opera. See also **Chá-pôm-chá-pôm**.

Auto-di-pau [‘awto di paw] *n*
Chinese play using wooden puppets.

Avanâ [ava’nạ] *vi*
To wave, fan oneself.

Avano [a’vạnu], **abano** [a’bạnu] *n*
Fan.

Avaria [ava’ria] *n*
1. Skill, talent.
2. Loss, trouble *Já buscâ avaria* he went looking for trouble.

Azêdo [a’zẹdu] *adj*
Tired, weak, shaky. *Dançâ até ficâ perna azêdo* to dance your legs off.

Azedado [azẹ’dadu] *adj*
Offended.

Azête-di-pau [a’zẹte di paw] *n*
Oil extracted from the seeds of the tung tree (*Aleurites fordii*), traditionally rubbed into boats and cloth for waterproofing and preservation.

Azinha [a’ziɲa] *adv*
Quickly. *Azinha-azinha* very quickly.

Babá [bą'bą] *n*
1. Boy.
2. Young boy.

Babachai [bąbą'čąi] *n* (<*Maq. babá* + *C. tsai*² 仔)
1. Small child.
2. Baby.

Babado [ba'bądu] *adj*
Enamoured, in love.

Baba-lua¹ ['bąba 'lua] *n*
Full moon.

Baba-lua² ['bąba 'lua] *adj*
Moon-faced.

Babanino [bąbą'ninu] *n* (<*Maq. babá* + *P. menino*).
Over-indulged child.

Babau [bą'bąu] *adj*
Disappointed. *Ficâ babau* or *comê babau* to be disappointed, suffer a disappointment, be frustrated.

Babo ['bąbu] *n*
Saliva. *Boca corê babo* to hanker after something.

Baboso [ba'bọzu] *n*
Bib.

Bacarâ [bąka'rą] *vi*
To apply too much make-up or face powder.

Bacarado [baka'radu] *adj*
1. Dusty.
2. Used to describe a heavily made-up woman.

Bacia [ba'sia] *n*
1. Basin.
2. Chinese gong, percussion instrument, old-fashioned metal basin. cymbols.
❖***Batê bacia*** [bą'tẹ ba'sia] to announce, call everyone's attention.

Badalâ [bąda'lą] *vi & vt*
1. To be very talkative.
2. To proclaim, gossip.

Bafâ¹ [bą'fą] *vt*
To suffocate, cook.
Bafâ pisunto [bą'fą pi'zuntu] to boil ham.

Bafâ[2] [bą'fạ] *n*

1. Domino piece.

2. Old Macanese game played by three people with a kind of domino.

Bafado [ba'fądu] *adj*

Stifling.

Pussâ bafado [pu'sạ ba'fądu] too tired even to breath.

❖ ***Voz bafado*** [voz ba'fądu] weak voice.

Bafassâ [bąfa'sạ] *vt* (<*P. abafar* + *assar*)

To stew, cook meat in a pot with a lid.

Porco bafassâ ['porku bąfa'sạ] pork loin stew.

Bafo ['bąfu] *n*

1. Breathing.

2. Air.

❖***Bafo cumprido*** ['bą fu kom'pridu] ou ***bafo di ade*** ['bąfu di'ạdi] used to describe a person who talks a lot and repetitively.

Bagáte [ba'gąti] *n*

1. Spell used to induce love. ***Largâ bagate*** [lar'ga ba'gąti] to bewitch somebody with this purpose, by means of a drink.

2. Fascination, charm.

Bagatiâ [bagati'ạ] *vt*

To cast a spell, subject to the effects of a charm or a tea served to entrap somebody.

Bagí [bą'ji] *n* (*M. wajek*)

Name of a candy in Macao, made of rice, coconut, milk and sugar.

Baiám [bąi'aŋ] *n*

Three-coloured amaranth (*Amarantaceae*), known as <*in*^{6} *chói*^{3} 莧菜> in Chinese.

Bajú [bą'ǰu] *n* (<*M. baju*)

As in ***cabaia-bajú*** [ka'bą'ya bą'ǰu]. Baggy fine white top with elbow-length sleeves which used to be worn by women at home.

Balâ [bą'lą] *vi*
1. To dance.
2. To swing.
❖ ***Balâ vai, balâ vêm*** [bą'lą vay bą'lą veŋ] to hurry to and fro.

Balancás [balaŋ'kąs] *n* (<*M. belankas*)
1. Fool, useless person.
2. Hindrance.
3. Horseshoe crab (*Limulus moluccanus*).

Baléu [bą'lęu] *n*
A small platform or wooden frame for carrying Chinese allegorical figures in funerals and in festive processions.
See also **Amui-baléu**.

Balichám [bali'čaŋ] *n* (<*M. belacang*)
Salty condiment prepared with very small, dried shrimps; essential ingredient in many Macanese dishes.
See also **Bicho-balichám**.

Balsa ['bąlsa] *n*
Wooden tub formerly used for bathing.

Bambinela [bambi'nęla] *n*
Wooden curtain rod.

Baniane [ban'yani] *n*
1. Vest formerly worn by men.
2. Cloth jacket, formerly worn at home or to sleep.

Bantú [ban'tu] *adj*
Short, stout.

Barafunda [bara'funda] *n*
Confusion, shouting.

Barafustâ [barafus'tą] *vt*
1. To burst in.
2. To complain, protest.

Baritina [bari'tina] *n*
Uniform, clothing.

Barba ['bąrba] *n*
1. Beard.
2. Candy made by melting raw sugar, pulling it into the shape of a beard and then dusting it in toasted flour.

Barbéro-ansiado [bar'bęru ansi'adu] *syn* ***Barbéro-bafado***.

Barbéro-bafado [bar'bęru ba'fadu] *n*
Brimming with curiosity, anxious, impatient to find out or spread any news.

Bariga [ba'riga] *n*
Belly, paunch. *Comê metade bariga* to eat less than could be eaten.
Bariga-duro [ba'riga 'duru] constipation.
Bariga grándi [ba'riga 'grandi] pregnant.
Bariga vantú [ba'riga van'tu] stomach upset.
See **Rê, *rê na bariga***.

Bariguda [bąri'guda] *adj*
Pregnant.

Bâs [bąs] *n* (<*Eng. bus*)
Bus, light truck or lorry. *Tudo dia sentâ bâs vai comprâ sôm* I take the bus every day to go shopping.

Basbáqui [bas'bąki] *adj*
Foolish, gawping.

Bassâ [bą'sạ] *vt*
To lower.
Bassâ cabeça [bą'sạ ka'bęsa] to bow one's head, until the chin touches the chest.
Bassâ ôlo [bą'sạ 'ọlu] to lower one's eyes in shame.

Basso ['bąsu] *prep*
Low.
Basso-Monte ['bąsu 'mọnti] the area around the Fortress of Our Lady of the Mount.
Basso-Guia ['bąsu 'gia] the area around Guia Hill.

Bataliám [batali'aŋ] *n*
Military battalion.

Batatada [bata'tada] *n*
Macao cake made with sweet potatoes, coconut and eggs.

Batata-doce [ba'tata 'dọci] *n*
Girl from mainland China.

Batê [bą'tę] *vt*
To beat.

❖***Batê asa*** [ba'tẹ 'aza] to go out, go away, beat a retreat.
❖***Batê bacia*** [ba'tẹ ba'sia] see **Bacia**.
Batê bolo [ba'tẹ 'bọlo] to bake cakes.
❖***Batê cabeça*** [ba'tẹ ka'bẹsa] to kowtow.
❖***Batê costela*** [ba'tẹ kus'tẹla] to thump somebody's back when hugging.
Batê ôlo [ba'tẹ 'ọlu] to blink.
❖ ***Batê pê*** [ba'tẹ pẹ] to tap one's foot to indicate disagreement or impatience.
Batê porta [ba'tẹ 'porta] to slam a door.
Batê rabicho [ba'tẹ ra'biču] to braid hair.
❖***Batê títi*** [ba'tẹ 'titi] to show anger by slamming down objects.

Bate-cú [bąte'ku] *n*
See **Bule-bule**.

Bate-pêto [bą'tẹ 'pẹtu] *n*
1. Fervent, excessively pious believer. See **Biato lap-chôk**.
2. Somebody who promises the world, and guarantees the results. Hypocrite.

Bática ['bątika] *n*
Metal basin or bowl.

Baul [bą'ul] *n*
Trunk, wooden chest with a curved lid.

Bazar [ba'ząr] *n* (<*Per. bazar*).
Market. *Vai bazar comprâ sôm* to go market to buy food.

Bebezaina [bebe'ząina] *n*
Drink, beverages.

Bebinca [bi'biŋka] *n*
Pudding, dessert.
Bebinca-lete [bi'biŋka 'lẹti] milk pudding.
Bebinca-nabo [bi'biŋka 'nąbu] savoury turnip cake made with rice flour and pork.
Bebinca-rábano [bi'biŋka 'rąbanu] dish made with *arôz pulú,* turnip and Chinese sausage. ***Bebinca-pulú*** [bi'biŋka pu'lu] sweet made

with *arôz pulú,* coconut and eggs.
Bebinca vantú [bi'biŋka van'tu] pudding that has failed to rise, due to an "ill wind".

Bêço ['bẹsu] *n*
Lip.
Pussâ beço [pu'sạ 'bẹsu] To pout.
See **Virâ béço**.

Belis [be'lis], **belis maroto** [be'lis ma'rotu] *n* (<*M. bilis*)
Whitebait (*Stolephorus Commersonii*), often used in Chinese food.

Belle-flower [bẹl 'flạwer] *n* (<*Fr. belle* + *Eng. flower*)
Tender woman, but heavy and slow.

Bêm [bẹŋ] *adv*
Well. *Fazê bem* to do good.
Bêm-pôsto [bẹŋ 'pọstu] well dressed, good-looking.
Bêm-di ['bẹŋdi] Very. *Êle tâ bêm-di filiz* he is very happy.
See **Di**, **Ui-di**.

Bêm-fêto [bẹŋ 'fẹto] *adv*
Well, correctly. *Êle papiâ português qui bêm-fêto* he speaks Portuguese well.

Bênça ['bẹŋsa] *n*
Blessing.

Bétele ['betle] *n* (<*Mal. vettila*)
Betel pepper leaf (*Piper betle*), which used to be chewed along with betel nut (**areca**). *Bétele vestido di casamento* a keepsake that used to be distributed to guests at weddings, made of betel nuts wrapped in betel pepper leaves.

Bezâ [bẹ'zạ] *vt*
To kiss.

Bêzo ['bẹzu] *n*
Kiss. See also **Ucho**.

Biato ['bi'ạtọ] *n*
Very pious person, superficially or genuinely.

Biato lap-chôc [‘bi’ątọ ląp ’čok] (<*beato* + *C. lab⁹jug⁷* (*vela*) 臘燭) *Lit.* a candlelighter, somebody whose devotions are only for show.

Biba [‘biba] *n* (<*C. pei⁴ pa⁴* 枇杷) Loquat. Fruit of the loquat tree (*Eriobotrya japonica*).

Bicho [‘biču] *n*

1. Bug. Any worm or insect.
2. Person, fellow, individual.
❖ ***Bicho-balichám*** [biču bali’čaŋ] restless person.
❖ ***Bicho careta, gato sapato*** [‘biču ka’ręta ‘gątu sa’pątu] despicable person of no importance.
❖ ***Bicho-carpintéro*** [biču karpin’tęru] fidget, somebody who cannot stay still for long.
❖ ***Bicho di festa*** [‘biču di ‘fęsa] party animal.
❖ ***Bicho-máto*** [biču ’mątu] stay-at-home.
❖ ***Mau bicho*** [mąw ‘biču] unreliable person.

Bicho-bicho [‘biču’biču] *n* Macanese candy, made of flour and eggs covered with caramelised sugar.

Bicho-dachim [‘bičuda’čiŋ] *n* A kind of dragonfly. When it flutters it wings, its tail moves up and down like the rod of a jeweller’s scales. See **Tachim**.

Bicho-mel [‘biču ’męw] *n* Bee.

Bicho-núne [‘biču ’nuni] *n* Dragonfly.

Bicho-saúde [‘biču sạ’udi] *n* Praying mantis.

Bife [‘bifi] *n*

1. Steak. Also used for chop. ***Bife pó bolacho*** [‘bifi pọ bo’ląču] steak milanese, or cutlet.
2. Englishman. ***Bifalhada*** a group of English people.

Bispo-di-galinha [‘bispu di ga’liɲa] *n*
Parson’s nose.

Bôbo [‘bọbu] *n*
1. Somebody who dresses up for Carnival, *syn* ***Bôbo di quarentora***.
2. Ridiculous person or situation.

Bobôi [bọ’bọi], **boibôi** [bọi’bọi] *vt*
To swing. *Bobôi quiança* to rock a child.

Boboriça [bọbọ’risa] *n*
Folly, nonsense. *Cala bóca, nê-bôm papiâ boboriça* be quiet, don’t talk nonsense. See *also* **Parabiça**.

Bóbra [‘bǫbra] *n*
Pumpkin.

Bóca [‘bǫka] *n*
Mouth.
Bóca aberto [‘bǫka ‘bertu] open-mouthed, amazed.
Bóca chacha [‘bǫka ‘čą’ča] old woman’s mouth.
❖ ***Bóca cherâ lete*** [‘bǫka ‘čẹ’rạ ‘lẹti] said of somebody who is green.
❖ ***Bóca di cano*** [‘bǫka di ‘kạnu] glutton.
❖ ***Bóca di sapo*** [‘bǫka di ‘sapu] big mouth.
❖ ***Bóca dóci*** [‘bǫka ‘dǫsi] sweet-talker, somebody who has an affected manner of speech.
❖ ***Bóca fino*** [‘bǫka ‘finu] gourmet, selective, somebody who only likes the finer things in life.
❖ ***Bóca fino-fino*** [‘bǫka finu’finu] sharp words offered in retort.
❖***Bóca grándi*** [‘bǫka ‘grandi] exaggerated, pompous, boastful.
❖***Bóca lála-lála*** [‘bǫka ‘lạla ’lạla] chatterbox.
Bóca patarata [‘bǫka pata’rąta] braggart, cheat.
❖***Bóca quente*** [‘bǫka ’kenti] soothsayer, person who foretells sad events.

❖ ***Bóca roto*** ['bǫka 'rǫto] a person who can't keep secrets.
❖ ***Bóca sujo*** ['bǫka 'suju] swearer.
Bóca-torto ['bǫka 'tǫrtǫ] grimace. *Fazê bóca-torto* to pull a face.

Bocarám [bǫka'raŋ] *n*
Street corner, exit of a public street.

Bode-vaca ['bǫdi 'vąka] *n*
Strong healthy lad, corpulent clumsy child. *Ado masquí têm catorze ano sã ung'a bode-vaca!* he's only fourteen and he's already a strapping lad. Also **bode-vêlo**.

Bode-vêlo ['bǫdi 'vẹlo] See **Bode-vaca**.

Bofatada [bofa'tada] *n*
1. A slap on the face. *Cara di panhâ bofatada* to look defiant, asking for trouble.
2. Instant, moment. *Ung'a bofatada já têm aqui* he arrived in a jiffy. See also **Pancada**.

Boiâ [bọ'ya] *vi*
To go out at night. To frequent night clubs.

Boiám [bu'yaŋ] *n*
Vat. Large clay receptacle for holding solids or liquid.

Boibôi [bọi'bọi] See **Bobôi**.

Bolacho [bo'ląču] *n*
Cookie, biscuit.
Pó-bolacho [pǫ bo'ląču] crumbs used in batter.

Bolo bate-pau ['bọlọ bąte 'pąw] *n*
Moon cake, eaten during mid-Autumn festival (15th day of the 8th month).

Bolo mármre ['bọlọ 'mąrmre] *n*
Marble cake, made with cocoa stirred into the mix to create a marbled effect.

Bolo minino ['bọlọ mi'ninu] *n*
Cake made with toasted coconut and ground biscuits, dusted with icing sugar.

Bolo nata [‘bọlọ ‘nạta] *n*
Egg tart.

Bolo supiám [‘bọlọ su’piaŋ] See **Supiám**.

Bolontrôm [bọlọn’trọŋ] See **Volontrôm**.

Bôm [bọŋ] *adv*
Good. *Más bôm* (i) better; (ii) worthwhile.
Bôm-sono [bọŋ’sọno] good night, have a good rest.

Boncô [boŋ’kọ] *adj & n* (<*M. bongkok*)
Humpback.

Boquizâ [boki’zạ] *vi*
To pronounce, say something.

Botâ [bọ’tạ] *vt*
1. To put, place. *Botâ vazo-fula na chám* to put the vase on the floor.
Botâ mesa [bọ’tạ ‘mẹza] to lay the table.
Botâ na fólia [bọ’tạ na‘fọlia] to place in the newspaper.
❖ ***Botâ faladura*** [bọ’tạ fala’dura] to give a speech.
❖***Botâ figura*** [bọ’tạ fi’gura] to show.
2. To set to.
Botâ corê [bọ’tạ‘ko’rẹ] to run off.
Botâ fuzí [bọ’tạ fu’zi] to run away.

Bote [‘bọ’te] *n*
Small rowing boat.

Botelha [bo’tẹλa] *n*
Bottle.

Botica [bo’tika] *n*
Shop.
Botica-mestre [bo’tika ‘mestri] Chinese pharmacy (*lit.* Apothecary of the Chinese healer). Place where medicinal concoctions and other Chinese medicines are sold.

Bói [bọi] *n* (<*Eng. boy*)
Waiter. *Chomâ bói trazê café co lête.*

Brajéro [bra’ǰẹro] See **Brejéro**.

Brêdo [ˈbrẹdo] *n*
Vegetable.
Brêdo raba-raba selection of cheap, poor quality vegetables. See **Raba-raba**.

Brejéro [breˈǰẹro] **brajéro** [braˈǰẹro] *n*
Philanderer, knave. *Estung'a vêlo-công ui-di bóca dóci, brejéro!* what a silver tongue that old man has! what a rascal!

Brigado [briˈgạdu], **obigado** [obiˈgadu] *adv*
Thankful, grateful.

Brinco [ˈbriŋku] *n*
1. Toy.
2. Game. *Nunca sã brinco,* this is not for playing.
3. Show, performance. *Dâ brinco* or *fazê brinco* to put on a show.

Bronco [ˈbrọŋko] *adj & n*
Stupid, idiot.

Bufutiâ [bufutiˈạ] *vt*
To slap.

Bule-bule [ˈbuli ˈbuli] *n*
Bird in the *Pycnonotidae* family.
Bule-bule batê-cu or *batê-cú* Bird in the *Motacillidae* family.

Bulí [buˈli] *vi & vt*
To move, interfere, provoke. *êle tâ bulí co iou* he's bothering me. *Nunca bôm bulí co iou-sua boca* don't provoke me and make me talk.
❖***Bulí fêmea*** [buˈli ˈfẹmia] to get involved with women.
❖***Bulí vêm bulí vai*** [buˈli vẹŋ buˈli vại] used to describe a restless person.

Bulicioso [bulisiˈọso] *adj*
1. Agitator, provoker.
2. Meddler, busy-body.

Bunitéza [buniˈtẹza] *adj*
1. Pretty.
2. Funny, obedient.

Bur-bur [burˈbur] *n*
Saltwater fish with no bones.

Buricido [buri'sidu] *adj & adv*
Boring, dull, unpleasant. *Qui buricido estung'a quiança!* what an annoying child!

Burifado [buri'fadu] *adj*
1. Impregnated.
2. Sprinkled, covered with. *Mínchi burifado co sutate* mince marinated in soy sauce.

Burumâ [buru'mạ] *vt*
1. To get close.
2. To hide.
3. To bore. *Sai daqui, vôs tâ burumâ iou-sa costa* go away, you are hurting my back (with your hands).

Buscâ [bus'kạ] *vt*
1.To search, look for. *Chacha tâ buscâ su oclo* grandpa is looking for his spectacles. *Quim vo-sotro tâ buscâ?* who are you looking for?
Buscâ sarna pa cuçâ [bus'kạ 'sạrna pa cu'sạ] to go looking for trouble.
2. To fetch.

Buzuntâ [buzun'tạ] *vt*
1. To grease.
2. To make dirty.
Mám buzuntado [maŋ buzun'tadu] greasy hands.
3. To cover with mud.

Cabaia [ka'baya] *n*
1. Chinese jacket.
2. Long Chinese tunic.
3. Windbreaker (sports jacket).

Cabeça [ka'bęsa] *n*
1. Head, mind.
Quebrâ cabéça [kę'brą ka'bęsa] (i) to dwell on one topic; (ii) to search for a solution to a problem.
❖***Cabéça di atum*** [ka'bęsa di a'tuŋ] trickster.
Cabeça-di-bonzo [ka'bęsa di 'bonzo] soup prepared in bain-marie using the skin of a winter gourd.
Cabéça-di-vento [ka'bęsa di 'vẹntu] forgetful, head in the clouds.
Cabéça-grándi [ka'bęsa 'grandi] (i) innovative. (ii) ringleader.
2. Chief, controller.
❖***Cabeça-di-cobra*** [ka'bęsa di 'kǫbra] snakehead, trafficker in illegal immigrants.
Cabeça-di-cúli [ka'bęsa di 'kuli] stevedore at the docks and markets responsible for a team of coolies.
Cabéça-di-hui [ka'bęsa di wi] person who chairs the meetings of the **hui**. See **Hui**.
❖***Cabeça-di-lorcha*** [ka'bęsa di 'lǫrča] captain of a boat.

Cabeçada [kabẹ'sada] *n*
Bowing the head so that the chin rests on the chest.
Dâ cabeçada [dą kabẹ'sąda] to nod off, head drooping.
Panhâ cabeçada [pą'ɲą kabẹ'sada] to suffer business setbacks.

Cabeçudo [kabẹ'sudu] *adj*
Stubborn, reluctant.

Cabelo-de-bonzo [ka'bẹlo di 'bonzo] *n*
Fibrous blackish seaweed used in many Chinese dishes, particularly in the vegetarian dish known as <**chái**>. Also used to make a jelly called **leong-fan**.

Cabêlo-noiva [ka'bẹlo 'nọiva] *n*
Sweet made with eggs and strands of sugar, reminiscent of golden hair.

Cabrám [ka'braŋ] *n*
1. Cuckold.
2. Boyfriend.
3. Lover.

Cabuz [ką'bus] See **pêsse cabús**.

Cacada [ką'kąda] *n*
Laughter. *Rí cacada* to split one's sides laughing.

Cacai [ką'kại] *adj* (<*Eng. cock-eyed*)
Cross-eyed. *Ôlo cacâi*, squint-eyed.

Cachaçám [kąča'saŋ] *n*
A whack on the back of the neck.

Cachí [ką'či] *vt* (<*M. kacip*)
1. To bite, bite through.
2. To chew.

Cáchi-báchi ['kači 'bąči], **cáchi-váchi** [kači 'vąči] *n* See **Raspiáti**.
Lowly person.

Cachipe [ka'čipi] *n* (<*M. kacip*)
Miser, avaricious person.

Cachipiâ [kačipi'ą] *vt* (<*M. kacip*)
1. To make oneself comfortable.
2. To squeeze.

Cachipiado [kačipi'ạdu] *adj* (<*M. kacip*)
1. Narrow.
2. Squashed.

Cáchi-váchi ['kači 'vąči] See **Cáchi-báchi**.

Cacho ['kąču] *n*
Large quantity. *Cacho-cacho di gente* a large crowd of people.

Cachôro[1] [ka'čọro] *adj*
1. Coward.
2. Ghastly.

Cachôro[2] [ka'čọro] *n*
Dog of any size. *Cachôrro-fêmea* bitch. *Cachôro morto* dead or useless dog.
Cachôro-china [ka'čọro 'čina] dog whose bark is worse than his bite.
Cachôro-doido [ka'čọro 'dọdo] rabid dog.

Cachupada [kaču'pada], [kašu'pada] *n*
Slap or pat on the neck. *Já dâ ung'a cachupada qui falâ misericórdia* he gave him such a whack that he begged for mercy.

Cacueta [kakw'ẹta] *n*
1. Defect in a person.
2. Person with a nervous tic.

Cacús [ką'kus] *n* (<*D. kakhuis*).
Toilet, latrine. Formerly, privy.

Cadacê [kada'sẹ], **cadecê** [kadẹ'sẹ] *adj & n*
1. Every.
2. Each one. *Cadacê sandê ung'a candia-céra* everybody lights a candle.
3. Anyone.

Cadera [ką'dẹra] *n*
1. Chair.
2. Sedan chair.
3. Lumbar region. *Doí cadera* (i) (lower) back ache; (ii) to have back ache.

Cadung'a [ka'duŋa] *syn* **Cadacê**.

Cafelâ [kąfẹ'lạ], **cafulâ** [kąfu'lạ] *vt*
To plaster a wall.

Cáfre ['kąfri] *n*
1. African.
2. Dark-skinned person.

Cafulâ [kąfu'lạ] See **Cafelâ**.

Cagám [ką'gaŋ] *adj & n*
Timid person, who is afraid of everything.

Cagarola [kaga'rọla] *adj & n*
Timid person.

Cai [kại] *vi*
1. To fall. *Já cai di cumprido na chám* he fell and lay sprawled on the floor.
2. To get carried away.
❖ ***Cai madre*** [kại 'mạdre] prolapse of the uterus.
Cai na asnéra [kại na as'nẹra] to get carried away by.
❖***Cai pê-mám*** [kại pẹ'maŋ] (i) to lose one's temper. (ii) to become disoriented.
❖ ***Cai na putau*** [kại na pu'taw] to commit a faux-pas.
Cai sin sintido [kại siŋ sin'tidu] (i) to faint. (ii) to swoon.

Caia ['kạia] *n*
Mosquito net hung over a bed like a tent.

Cai chuva [kại 'čuva] *v*
To rain. *Azinha vai casa-ia, lôgo cai chuva* let's get home quickly because it's going to rain.

Cai sol [kại sọl] *v*
To grow dark.

Cajám [ka'ǰaŋ] *n* (<*M. kajang*)
Fan made with a kind of palm leaf.

Cajola [ka'ǰọla] *n*
Bird-cage.

Calâ-bóca! [kạ'lạ 'bọka] *v*
To be silent. *Calá-boca!* shut up!

Calado-calado [ka'lạdu ka'lạdu] *adv*
Stealthily.

Calabôço [kalạ'bọsu] *n*
Prison.

Calça-ganga ['kạlsa 'gạnga] *n*
Demin shorts for boys.

Calçám [kạl'saŋ] *n*
Trousers, shorts. *Calçám cumprido* long trousers.

Calça-moura ['kạlsa 'mọura] *n*
Light trousers worn by men at home or in bed.

Cális [‘kąlis], [‘kąliš] *n*
Wine-glass. *Tóne tâ bebê ung’a cáliz di vinho-Porto* Tóne is having a glass of Port.

Calisto! [ką’listo] *interj*
Misfortune. *Qui calisto!* bad luck!

Cám [kaŋ] *n*
Dog. See also **cachôro**.
❖ ***Ferâ cám*** [fę’rą kaŋ] to swindle.

Camalenga [kama’lęŋga] *n*
Winter gourd. *Dóci camalenga* preserve made with gourd, sugar and fig leaves.

Cambaláncho [kamba’ląɲču] *n*
1. Gang.
2. Riff-raff, rabble.

Cambiâ [kambi’ą] *vt*
To change, alter. *Cambiâ sapeca* to exchange money.

Camarám [kama’raŋ] See **cambrám**.

Cambrám [kam’braŋ], **camarám** [kama’raŋ] *n*
Shrimp. *Bôlo di cambrám* prawn dumpling.
Cambrám mizóna [kam’braŋ mi’zǫna] mantis shrimp (*Harpiosquilla raphidea, Squilla raphidea*). Called *lai-liu h’á* in Chinese.

Cam-cám [kaŋ’kaŋ] *adj & adv* (<*M. kang kang*)
Arched, legs akimbo. *Andâ perna cam-cám* to walk bow-legged.

Cam-cho-lám [kam čo ’ląm] See **Lám**.

Camsé [kam’sę] *n* (<*C. kam*^{1} *se*^{2} 金捨)
1. Tip, reward, alms.
2. Cash bribe.

Camiám [kąmi’aŋ] *n*
1. Lorry.
2. Bus.

Camisa-mêa [ka’miza ’mẹa] *n*
Cotton undershirt.

Campa [‘kąmpa] *n*
Doorbell. *Iou-sa casa têm ung’a campa qui bunito* my doorbell is very nice.

Campenha [kam’pęɲa] See **Campa**.

Canalhám [kana’ʎaŋ] *adj & n*
Rascal, scoundrel, knave.

Canarim [kana’riŋ] *n*
Indian, usually Christian, from former Portuguese India.

Cancaná [kaŋka’ną] *n*
Bracelets, bangles.

Cancôm [kaŋ’kǫŋ] *n*
Water spinach (*Ipomoea aquatica*). Called <*tong¹ choi³* 通菜> in Chinese.

Candia [kan’dia] *n*
Oil lamp.
“Candia” cera [kan’dia ‘cera] wax candle.

Canecám [kanę’kaŋ] *n*
Tankard.

Canga-pêlo [‘kaŋga ’pęlu] *n*
Cotton cloth.

Canje [kaɲ’ǰi] *n*
1. Chicken broth.
2. Any kind of broth with rice.
Canje brânco watery boiled rice.
Canje fula papaia broth made from papaya blossom.

Cantinela [kanti’nęla] *n*
Song.

Cao-miáng! [kąu mi’aŋ] *adv*
(<*C. kao³ meang⁶* 救命)
Scream for help.

Cap [kąp] *n*
Basket for carrying fish, used when fishing. *Quelóra vai pesca amestê levâ cap* you have to take a **cap** when you go fishing.

Capa [‘kąpa] *n*
Lady’s winter coat.

Capa-dóci [kąpa’dǫsi] *n*
1. Helpful person.
2. Female know-all.

Capa-pêlo [ʻkąpa ʼpęlo] *n*
Fur coat.

Capám [kąʼpaŋ] *n*
1. Capon, neutered cock.
2. Useless person. *Se pôde, sâm capaz, si nôm pôde sâm capám* if you can, you're smart, if you can't, you're useless.

Capaz [kąʼpąs] *adj*
1. Know-all.
2. Intelligent.
3. Well-taught.
4. Capable, daring. *Si sâm capaz* if you dare. *Iou nunca capaz* I wouldn't dare.

Capí [kaʼpi] *vt* (<*M. gapek*)
To get caught, squeeze. *Capí mám na porta* he caught his hand in the door.
Capí ôlo [kaʼpi ʻǫlu] to wink.
Capí mám [kaʼpi ʻmaŋ] to wave.
Capí pâm co pisunto [kaʼpi pąŋ ku piʼzuntu] to make a ham sandwich.

Capido [kąʼpidu] *adj*
Pressed, narrow.
Rabo capido [ʻrąbo kąʼpidu] to rest uneasy, know one is guilty.

Capotám [kapoʼtaŋ] *n*
Big cloak.

Capote [kaʼpǫti] *n*
1. Overcoat.
2. Lady's long overcoat.

Captan [ʻkęptąn] *n* (<*Eng. captain*)
Head waiter in a restaurante, cafe or on a ship.

Cáqui [ʻkąki] See **Figo cáqui**.

Cará [kaʼrą] *n* (<*M. karat*)
Crust. Hard dry residue at the bottom of the pot.

Cara [ʻkąra] *n*
Face.
Bôm cara [bǫŋ ʻkąra] good-looking, pleasant features.

Cara chapado [‘kąra čapądu] spitting image.
Cara di cu [‘kąra di ku] twit.
Cara di merda [‘kąra di’mędra] very ugly.
Cara di putau [‘kąra di pu’tąw] stupid-looking, cretin.
Cara di quim deve nunca paga [‘kąra di’kiŋ ‘dęvi ‘nuŋka ‘pąga] scrounger.
Cara di rato cheroso [‘kąra di ’rątu čę’rǫzu] insidious person.
Cara limpo [kąra’limpo] honest, clear conscience.
Cara machucado [‘kąra mačuʼkądu] ugly person with assymetrical features, whose face looks as if it has been squashed.
Dâ cara [dą ’kąra] to “give face”, to respect.
Olâ cara [ǫ’lą ‘kąra] to look at somebody’s face.

Carambola [karam’bǫla] *n*
Star fruit (*Averrhoa carambola*).

Careta [ka’ręta] *n*
1. Car. *Careta dôdo* fast car.
2. Any vehicle.
3. Grimace, frown. *Fazê careta* to grimace.

Careta-fiado [ka’ręta fi’ądu] *n*
Spool of thread.
❖ ***Cintura di careta-fiado*** [sin’tura di ka’ręta fi’ądu] hourglass figure.

Carí [ka’ri] *n*
Curry. *Carí di môro* Indian curry.

Cartâ [kąr’tą] *vt*
1. To carry. *Cartâ vai* to take. *Cartâ vêm* to bring.
Cartâ levâ [kąr’tą lę’vą] (i) to take messages. (ii) to bring news.
2. To be pregnant. *Jêto qui tâ cartâ* appearance of being pregnant.

Casamento-di-macaco [kasa’mentu di ma’kaku] *n*

Unusual weather, when it rains and shines at the same time.

Casarám [kąza'raŋ] *n*
Mansion.

Cási ['kazi] *adv*
Almost.

Catá-cutí [ką'tạ ku'ti] *n* (<*M. katah* + *kuti*)
Knick-knacks, bits and pieces.

Catapú [kąta'pu] *n* (<*Eng. catapult*)
Catapult.

Catavénto [kąta'vęntu] *n*
Chameleon, person who shifts from one opinion, party or group to another as it suits him or her.

Cate ['kąti] *n* (<*M. kati*)
Chinese weight, equivalent to 604 grams. One catty consists of 16 taels, one hundred catties make a picul.

Categuizâ [kategi'zạ] *vi & vt*
1. To catechize.
2. To try to convince.

Catiaca [kati'ąka] *n* (<*M. ketiak*)
Armpit. *Fêde catiaca* body odor from armpits.

Catravada [kątra'vąda] *n*
Group of people, usually from the same family. *Cartâ na tudo sa catravada vêm* to bring the clan along.

Catupá [kątu'pą] *n* (<*M. ketupat*)
Savoury Chinese cake made from rice, pork and other ingredients, and called <*ham*^{4} *iok*^{9} *chong*^{3} 咸肉粽> in Chinese.

Caurí [kąu'ri] *adj*
Chequered, speckled, used to decribe poultry.

Cavâ [ką'vạ] *adv & vt*
1. Later, afterwards.
2. To finish, end. *Alina já cavâ fazê trabalo casa* Alina has

already done her homework. See also **Ramatâ**.

Cavaquista [kava'kista] *adj*
Highly susceptible, easily frightened. See ***dâ cavaco***.

Caxám [ka'šaŋ] *n*
1. Big box, crude chest.
2. Funeral casket.
Caxám-terno [ką'šaŋ 'ternu] woven bamboo Chinese "wedding" basket.

Cegónha [sẹ'gọɲa] *n*
1. Stork.
2. Female nightsoil collector.
3. Female lover. *Istupôr di Secundino, tudo dia chegâ na casa assí tarde, certo têm cegonha* that idiot Secundino is late home every day. He must have a lover!

Cén [sẹn] *num* (*<Eng. cent, centavo*)
One-hundredth of a pataca, one *avo*.

Cento ['sẹnto] *num*
One hundred. *Uncento* (i) a hundred; *Uncento fora* a hundred-odd. (*Un*) *cento pataka fora* a hundred-odd patacas. (ii) one hundred. *Quánto cento* hundreds, several hundred. (iii) many, an amount. *Tâ papiâ um cento pantominice* you're telling a stack of lies. *Cartâ uncento livro vêm casa* he brought a pile of books back home.

Cerâ [sẹ'rạ] *vt*
1. To polish the floor or furniture. *Cerâ chám* to wax the floor.
2. To close, enclose.

Cerâ-dente [sẹ'rạ 'dente] *v*
To clench one's teeth in anger. *Nê-bôm cerâ dente* calm down, don't get worked up.

Ceróla [sẹ'rọla] *n*
Long johns.

Cerzí [ser'zi] *vt*
To darn, mend.

Chá [čą] *n*
1. Plant in the tea family.
2. Infusion made with tea leaves.
3. Infusion of medicinal plants. *Chá di hortelám di sopa* mint tea, for rheumatic pains, indigestion or worms.
Chá di pêlo-pê infusion to ward off frights. *Chá di peso* infusion to protect against indigestion or stomach-ache. *Chá seng kap* Chinese medicinal infusion.
❖ ***Chá gordo*** [čą 'gordu] festive high tea.

Chacarâ [čąka'rạ] *vt* (<*M. cekak, cekak*)
1. To embrace.
2. To suffocate.

Chácha[1] ['čąča] *n* (<*M. cacah*)
Dessert made with mung beans, tapioca, yam, coconut and raw sugar.

Chácha[2] ['čąča] *n*
1. Grandmother.
2. Old woman. *Chácha-chácha* old ladies. *Rópa di chácha* old lady's dress. *Chácha di casa* the most elderly lady in a family.
3. Respect shown to old ladies.

Cha-cháu ['ča'čąu] See **Chau-chau**.

Chachini [čači'ni] *n*
Macanese dish prepared with flaked fish cooked in coconut milk and chilli.

Chado ['čądọ] *adj* (<*M. cadek,* <*Conc. chyad*)
1. Smart, intelligent.
2. Skilful.

Chai-fêng [čąi'fẹŋ] *n* (<*C. tsai*^{1} *feng*^{2} *猜??*), (<*C. tsai*^{4}*kün*^{4} *猜拳*)
"Paper, scissors, stone", a popular method for drawing lots or deciding order, used by two or three players before starting a game. Simultaneously, the players display one of three hand symbols representing either

paper (open hand), stone (closed fist) or scissors (fist with index and middle fingers extended). Paper wins against stone because it can wrap it up, stone wins against scissors because it blunts the blade, and scissors win against paper because they can cut it.

Chalaçâ [čala'sạ] *vi*
1. To joke.
2. To talk animatedly.

Chalâ-chalâ [čą'lạ čą'lạ] *adj*
Dishevelled, dirty, umkempt. *Êla sâm ung'a Maria chalâ chalâ* she looks very unkempt.

Cháli[1] ['čąli] *n*
Shawl, usually made of wool, and commonly used by the ladies of Macao in winter.

Cháli[2] ['čąli] *n (<Mar./Kon tçal)*
Small, narrow street, alleyway.

Chaminica [čami'nika] *n*
1. Small teacup with no handle, used in Chinese restaurants.
2. Clay dish, formerly used as a mold for homemade cakes.

Champaca [čam'pąka] *n*
Magnolia, a fragrant white (*Michelia champaca*) or yellow (*Michelia alba*) flower.

Champorâ [čampọ'rạ] See **Champurâ**.

Champurâ [čampu'rạ], **champorâ** [čampọ'rạ] *vt (<M. campur)*
To mix. *Champurâ vaca com brêdo* Beef and vegetable stir-fry.

Chanquêm [čaŋ'kẹŋ] *n (<C. chon*[4] *keng*[2] *巡警)*
Chinese policeman.

Chapâ [čą'pạ] *vt*
1. To join, lean (against). *Chapâ assento* to tilt a chair, sit down. *Intrâ, chapâ assento* come in and sit down. *Chapâ perto* to lean. *Chapâ perto di*

noiva to snuggle up to one's girlfriend.

❖***Chapâ calo*** [čą'pą 'kalu] to ask for a loan.

❖***Chapâ na umbigo*** [čą'pą na um'bigu] to be very clingy.

❖***Chapâ mám*** [čą'pą maŋ] (i) to marry; (ii) to shake hands.

2. To spit. *Chapâ fio* to thread a needle.

❖***Chapâ prêgo*** [čą'pą 'pregu] to pawn.

Chapadeca [čapa'dęka] *n*

A Chinese girl with a flat face.

Chapado [ča'padu] *adj*

1. Leaning. *Chapado na corpo* leaning into somebody.

2. Flat. *Nariz chapado* snub-nosed.

Maquista chapado [ma'kista ča'padu] true Macanese.

Chapéu [ča'pęu] *n*

1. Hat. *Chapéu-côco* bowler hat, formerly used by men with a certain social status.

2. Cap.

Chapéu-de-padre [ča'pęu di 'pądri] prawn dumpling shaped like a cardinal's birretta. Called <*há[1] kau[2] 蝦餃*> in Cantonese.

Chá-pom-chá-pom [ča'pọŋ ča'pọŋ] *n* (<*M. cak pong-pong*)

1. Clash of the cymbols in Chinese orchestras and bands.

2. Classical Chinese drama accompanied by a traditional orchestra.

Chap-sio [čap'siw] *n* (<*C. tsa[1] sio[1] 叉燒*)

Barbecued pork.

Cháqui-cháqui ['čąki 'čąki] *adv*

With the excuse of.

Chareta [čą'ręta] *n* (<*T. chiratta*)

1. Ladle made from half a coconut shell with a wooden handle. *Cholê água co chareta* to take water out of a receptacle with a *chareta*.

2. Buttocks, behind. *Olôtro já cortâ saia atê chareta* her skirt is slit right up her thighs.

Chatôm [ča'tọŋ] *n* (<*C. tsa⁴ tong²* *茶桶*)
Cushioned hamper for holding a teapot.

Châu [čąw] *n* (<*C. tsau⁴* *綢*)
Pongee garments worn by lowly Chinese women in Macao such as household servants and tanka women.

Chau-cháu [čąw'čąw], **cha-cháu** [čą'čąw] *n* (<*C. tsau²* *炒*)
1. Chinese stew, usually made of a mixture of meats and vegetables.
Chau-chau pêle Macanese stew made with ingredients stewed in lard. See also **Tacho**.
Chau-min [čąw'min] stewed noodles, often served with beef or pork.
2. Miscellany.
3. Mess, confusion, disorder.

Chau-chau-lau-lau [čąw'čąw ląw'ląw] *n* (<*Maq. chau-chau* + *M. lauk*).
Mess, confusion, disorder.
Ung'a chau-lau-lau-lau nâ-mas! this is a total mess!

Chegâ [čẹ'gạ], [šẹ'gạ] *vt*
1. To arrive. *Já chegâ tarde vai siviço* he got to work late.
2. To be enough. *Nadi chegâ sapeca* it's not enough money.
3. To approach, get near. *Nôm pôde chegâ mám* he can't stretch that far.
4. To be as much as, compare to, be on a par with. *Títi nôm pôde chegâ iou corê* my aunt cannot run as fast as I.

Chengcau [čẹŋ'kạu] *n* (<*C. tseng³ kau³* *正教*)
Chinese convert to Catholicism. Often used derogatively, to mean somebody useless.

Cherâ [čẹ'rạ] *vt*
To smell.
❖***Cherâ-córda!*** [čẹ'rạ 'kọrda] get lost!
❖ ***Cherâ fundilho di padre*** [čẹ'rạ fun'diλu di 'pạdri] used to describe an excessively pious woman.

❖ ***Cherâ fundilho di sógra!*** [čẹ'rạ fun'diλu di 'sọgra] *syn* ***Cherâ-corda!***

❖ ***Cherâ sôk sôk*** [čẹ'rạ sọk'sọk] sweating at the armpits. See also ***Fêde sôk sôk***.

❖ ***Cherâ vento*** [čẹ'rạ 'vẹntu] to have no food.

Cherám [čẹ'rạŋ] *n*
Spices.

Cherindê [čerin'dẹ] *n* (<*M. cirindit*)
Person who repeatedly asks for something. See also **Pedente**.
Maria Cherindê bird whose repeated call is supposed to augur rain.

Chêro [čẹro] *n*
Smell. *Chêro di catiaca* the smell of sweat from the armpits.
Agu-chêro perfume.

Cherôso [čeʼrọzu] *adj*
Fragrant, perfumed.

Chicalíli [čika'lili] *n*
Lily.

Chichai [či'čại] See **Chuchai**.

Chico ['čiku] *adj & n prop*
1. Diminutive of Francisco.
2. Gossip.

Chicorí [čikọ'ri], **chocorí** [čọkọ'ri] *vt*
1. To flirt, fool around in order to attract attention. *Chicha qui di garida, tâ chicorí co êle* Chicha is flirting with him.
2. To woo a woman.
3. To court.
4. To have a sexual relationship.

Chicote [či'kọti] See **Fijám chicote**.

Chicú [či'ku] *n*
Tuber in the *Sagittaria trifolia* family. Also called **nhame chicú**.

Chilicate [čili'kạti] *n* (<*M. celekati* <*T. siri-katti*)

Small pliers used to crack open betel nuts.

Chilicóte [čili'kǫti] *n*
Croquet made with mince. ***Chilicote-fólia*** chilicote made of puff pastry.

Chíli-missó ['čili mi'sǫ] *n*
Spicy Chinese condiment made with chilli, vinegar and soybean paste. Called *<lát^{9} chiu^{1} cheong^{3}* 辣椒漿> in Chinese.
See **Missó**.

Chíli-mosquito ['čili mǫs'kitu] *n*
Cayenne pepper (*Capsicum frutescens*).

Chíli-ponta-céu ['čili 'ponta sęu] *n*
1. Kind of chilli which curves upwards, towards the sky.
2. Used to describe pert breasts.

Chimpâ [čim'pą] *vt*
1. To beat.
2. To shoot. *Já chimpâ nele di bem!* he has sounded off!

China ['čina] *n*
Chinese. *China-china* Chinese. See also **Náchi**.
❖ ***Cám china*** ['kaŋ 'čina] See ***Cachôro-china***.
China di lête ['čina di 'lęte] dairyman.
China falâ ['čina fą'lą] as the Chinese say. *China falâ, <mou^{5} man^{6} tai^{4}* 冇問題> as the Chinese say, <no problem!>
China pobre ['čina 'pǫbri] beggar.
❖ ***China-merenda*** ['čina me'ręnda] Chinese snack-seller.
China-rico ['čina 'riku] Chinese magnate.
Téra-china ['tęra 'čina] mainland China.

Chincha ['činča] *n* (<*M. cincang*)
The filling of a cake or pie.

Chinchám [čiŋ'čaŋ] *adj* (<*M. cincang*)
Crushed. *Corê-corê, escoregâ cai chinchám na chám mulado*

he fell while he was running and crashed onto the ground.

Chinela [či'nęlą] *n*
Slipper. *Usâ chinela vai rua* to go out in slippers.

Chintôi [čin'tọi] *n* (<*C. tsin*[1] *toi*[1] 煎堆)
Chinese fritter shaped like a ball, stuffed with prawns and rolled in sesame seeds.

Chip-chip [čip 'čip] *adj* (<*M. cipir*)
Blinking. *Ôlo chip-chip* sleeping, with drooping eyes.

Chipí [či'pi] *vt* (<*M. cipir*)
1. To touch.
2. To squeeze. To knead. ***Chipido cachipiado*** [či'pidu kačipi'ądu] tight, stuck.
❖***Chipí cherâ*** [či'pi če'rą] (i) to examine in great detail. *Siára-siára quelóra comprâ sôm têm qui chipi-cherâ tudo ancuza* when women go shopping they look at everything in detail. (ii) used to describe somebody who likes to know everything in detail.
3. To make narrow.

Chipido [či'pidu] *adj* (<*M. cipir + P. -do*)
Narrow, tight. *Travessa chipido* narrow alleyway. *Rópa chipido na corpo* tight dress.

Chipim [či'piŋ] *adj*
Tied, fastened. Used only in the expression ***pê chipim***, a reference to the bound feet of Chinese women, in contrast to ***pê solto***, a normal foot that has not been bound.

Chipizaina [čipi'ząina] *n* (<*M. cipir + P. -zaina*)
Indecent groping.

Chiquí [či'ki] *vt* (<*M. cekek*)
1. To strangle. *Estung'a quiança já chiquí galinha* this child strangled the hen.
2. To squeeze. *Chiquí tripa* to tighten one's belt.

Chiquía [či'kia] *n*

1. Braid or bun formerly used by women to show their marital status. *Marâ chiquía* to put one's hair up.

2. Chinese shuttlecock consisting of a cylindrical base made of layers of cardboard stuck together, and a bunch of feathers. Called <*in*[1] *chi*[1] *胭脂*> in Chinese.

3. Children's game that consists of throwing the **chiquía** up into the air and keeping it up for as long as possible.

Chirí [či'ri] *vi* (<*M. cirik*)

To wet oneself.

Rí qui chirí [ri ki či'ri] to laugh until bursting.

Chiribito [čiri'bitu] *n* (<*M. cirit-birit*)

1. Small child, stripling.

2. Sickly, fragile person.

Chirifada [čiri'fada] *n*

Diarrhoea, the trots.

Chiripâ [čiri'pạ] *vi* (<*T. cherippu*)

To stamp or clack with clogs.

Chiripo [či'ripu] *n* (<*T. cherippu*)

1. Clog

2. A pair of clogs.

Chíscate! [čiskati] interj

Interjection expressing surprise.

Chisco ['čisko] *n*

Devil, demon.

Chiste ['čisti] *n* (<*Sp. chiste*)

Natural fun. *Fazê chiste* to poke fun, joke, make fun of oneself. *Fazê pa chiste* to get a laugh. *Chiste qui nôm-têm chiste* joke that falls flat.

Chistoso [čis'tọso] *adj & n*

1. Funny.

2. Pleasant, nice.

3. Attractive. *Nhónha chistosa* attractive woman.

Chi-su [či'su] *n* (<*C. chi*[2] *sou*[1] *紫蘇*)
Figwort, medicinal plant (*Scrophularia nodosa*).

Chito[1] ['čito] *n* (<*Hin chitthi‹*)
1. Writing, letter, note.
2. Pawn chit.

Chito[2] ['čito] *n*
Nickname given to somebody short in stature.

Chivit [či'vit] *n*
Small bird in the *Sylviidae* family.

Chocâ [čọ'kạ] *vi*
1. To hatch, incubate.
2. To irritate, annoy.

Chocado [čọ'kạdu] *adj*
Irritated, fed up. *Pai tâ chocado co êle* dad is fed up with him. *Vós tâ fazê iou chocado* you're beginning to get on my nerves.

Chocolhâ [čọkọ'λạ] *vt*
To shake, tremble, vibrate.

Chocorí [čokọ'ri] See **Chicorí**.

Chofé [čọ'fẹ] *n* (<*Eng.*, <*F. chauffeur*)
Chauffeur.

Cholê[1] [čo'lẹ] *vt* (<*M. colek, mencolek*)
1. To spoon out of a recipient.
2. To thump, strike. *Já cholê êle di bem*, I thumped him.

Cholê[2] [čo'lẹ] *vt* (<*M. colek*)
To tap somebody.

Cholido [čo'lidọ] *adj*
Interfering, meddlesome. *Ficâ cholido* (i). To interfere; (ii) to be accused of interfering.

Chomâ [čọ'mạ] *vt*
1. To call. *Chomâ iou* or *chomâ pa iou* call me.
2. To be called. *Iou chomâ Maria* my name is Maria.

Choncâ [čọŋ'kạ] *vt* (<*C. tsong*[6] *揰* + *P. chocar*)
To collide, knock, coincide with *Ung'a careta já choncâ*

na otrung'a a car bumped into another vehicle.

Chonto ['čọntu] *n*
Great quantity. *Chicho fichâ ano, já convidâ ung'a chonto di genti* Chico invited a lot of people to his birthday party.

Chop [čọp] *n* (<*Eng. chop*)
1. Official license.
2. Student slang to indicate an absent lecturer, recorded with a stamp in a register.

Chubí [ču'bi] *vt* (<*M. cubit*)
1. To pinch. *Qui-foi chubí iou?* Why are you pinching me? *Já chubí braço* he pinched my arm.
2. To break off a piece of bread, cake or to pick off the petals of a flower. *Chubí pâm* to break bread into pieces.

Chubidela [čubi'dęla] *n* (<*M. cubit*)
Pinch.

Chuchai [ču'čại], **chichai** [či'čại] *n* (<*C. chu[1] chai[2] 豬仔*)
Chinese worker or coolie that set sail for central America from Macao and other harbours in South China.

Chúcho ['čuču] *adj & n* (<*M. cucok*)
Interfering, meddler.

Chuchú [ču'ču] *vt* (<*M. cucok*)
To roast on a spit, drive in. *Chuchu pau na chám* to drive a stick into the ground. *Chuchú pê na buraco,* trip on a hole in the ground.
❖***Chuchú bico*** [ču'ču 'biku] used to describe somebody sleepy, who has to keep their eyes open.

Chuchumeca [čuču'męka] *n* (<*M. cucok* + *Eng. maker*).
Troublemaker, busybody.

Chuchupa [ču'čupa] *n*
Paper poke used to sell roast peanuts or chestnuts. *Já comprâ ung'a chuchupa di façám* I bought a packet of peanuts.

Chumbâ [čum'bạ] *vi*
To become a fixture, used to describe somebody who settles down somewhere and then becomes very difficult to shift; to not give up. *Chumbâ na cadera* said of a guest who has overstayed his welcome.

Chunambeiro [čunạm'bẹirọ], [čunạm'bẹrọ] n
Oven for making **chunambo**.

Chunambo [ču'nạmbọ] *n*
Lime obtained from shells.

Chupâ [ču'pạ] *vt*
1. To suck.
❖ ***Chupâ dêdo*** to suck one's thumb, be left with nothing.
❖ ***Chupâ ôvo*** [ču'pạ 'ọvo], ***chupâ chíli*** [ču'pạ 'čili], or ***chupâ leng-kok*** [ču'pạ lẹŋ'kọ] get lost!
❖ ***Chupâ grog*** See ***Dále grog***.
2. To absorb.

Chupéta [ču'pẹta] *n*
Baby's bottle. Pacifier.

Chupou! [ču'pọ] *interj*
Expression used when somebody has been left speechless. *Chupou di bem!* He took it straight in the face!

Churâ [ču'rạ] *vt*
To weep, wail.
Churâ lágri curto-comprido [ču'rạ 'lągri 'kurtu kọm'pridu] to weep inconsolably.

Churado [ču'rạdu] *adj*
Melted, liquefied.

Churuto [ču'ruto] *n*
Cigar.

Chuva ['čuva] *n*
Rain. *Cai chuva* to rain.
Chuva filo-filo ['čuva 'filu 'filu] drizzle.
Chuva fino-fino ['čuva 'finu 'finu] light rain.
Chuva pedra ['čuva 'pẹdra] hail.

Cifâ [si'fạ] See **Cifrâ**.

Cifrâ [si'frạ], **cifâ** [si'fạ] *vt*
1. To clench.

2. To reveal one's teeth when laughing. *Cifrâ dente* to bare one's teeth in anger.
Cifâ dente! [si'fạ 'dẹnte] go away, don't bother me!
See also **Cerâ, *Cerâ dente***.

Cifrada [si'frạda] *n*
Race. *Ung'a cifrada já vai cozinha* she raced to the kitchen.

Cilicário [sili'kạriu] *n* (<*M. serikaya*)
Old Macanese sweet.

Cinematógrafo [sinẹma'tọgrafu] *n*
Cinema, screening room.

Cioso [si'ọso] *n*
Meddler, provoker.

Cissí [si'si] *vt* (<*M. sisil*)
1. To raise, lift (up).
2. To pull up. *Cissí calçám* to pull one's trousers up.

Ciumidade [siumi'dạdi] *n*
Jealousy. *Êle tâ atacado di ciumidade* he is overcome with jealousy.

Clareza [kla'rẹza] *n*
Explanation. *Dâ clareza* to explain, clarify, *syn* **Clariâ**.

Clariâ [klari'ạ] *vt*
To make clear.

Clu-clu [klu'klu] *n*
Onomatopæic word. Gambling game in which two dice are shaken inside a china cup covered with a saucer, creating the sound which gives it its name.

Co [ko] *conj & prep*
1. And. *Iou co vôs* you and I.
2. With. *Iou vai juntado co êle* I'm going with him. *Vôs pôde priguntâ co êle* you can ask him.

Coâ [kọ'ạ] *vt*
To filter, strain.
❖***Mizâ coâ*** [mi'zạ kọ'ạ] used to describe an extremely penny-pinching person, who

would even strain urine to get some use out of it.

Cobertô [kọbert'ọ] *n*
Lid of a pot or other recipient.

Cocôi [kọ'kọi] *vt* (<*C. mọ[1] kôi*)
To carry on one's back. To bear. *Mai tâ cocôi filo* the mother carried her son on her back.

Cojut [kọ'ǰut] *adj*
Lowlife. *syn* **Cudum**.

Colau [kọ'lạu] See **Culau**.

Cólcha ['kọlča] *n*
1. Bedcover.
2. Blanket or quilt. *Cólcha-papa* heavy quilt. *Cólcha-pena* feather quilt.

Colê-garfo [co'lẹ 'gạrfu] *n*
Spoon and fork. Cutlery. *syn* **Faca-garfo**.

Côlo ['kọlu] *n & vt*
1. Lap.
2. To sit on one's knee, carry.
❖ ***Côlo-mám côlo-pê*** ['kọlu maŋ'kọlu pẹ] idle.

Columbrâ [kolum'brạ] *vt*
1. To covet.
2. To have great expectations.

Comê [kọ'mẹ] *vt*
To eat.
❖ ***Comê babáu*** [kọ'mẹ ba'bạu] to be disappointed, disillusioned.
❖***Comê negâ*** [kọ'mẹ ne'gạ] to reap a benefit but not acknowledge it.
Comê qui ravirâ [kọ'mẹ ki rạvi'rạ] to gorge.
Comê qui sentâ ôlo [kọ'mẹ ki sẹn'tạ 'ọlu] to glut oneself. Note: <ôlo> here refers to **ôlo déco**.
Comê ramatâ [kọ'mẹ rạma'tạ] to eat everything up.

Comédia [ko'mẹdia] *n*
Review, comic play traditionally staged during Carnival.

Comezaina [kọme'zạina] *n*
Heavy meal.

Comoa [kọ'mọa] *n*
Bilge, formerly located outside the house.

Companhâ [kompa'ɲạ] *vt*
1. To accompany, follow. *Companhâ procissám* to join a procession. *Companhâ morto* to attend a wake. *Companhâ iou vai missa* go with me to mass.
2. To accompany, keep company. *Companhâ doente* to keep a patient company.

Compradô [kompra'dọ] *n*
1. Trusted servant responsible for doing the household shopping and for contracting and supervising the other servants.
2. Commissioner on board a ship.

Compridám [kumpri'daŋ] *n*
Length, extension.

Condorim [kọndọ'riɲ] *n* (<*M. kanduri*).
Old unit of weight, a one hundredth of a tael.

Confêto [koŋ'fẹtu] *n*
1. Confectionary.
2. Sweetie.

Consolâ [kọnsọ'lạ] *vt*
To comfort.

Consumí [kọnsu'mi] *vt*
1. To consume.
2. To mortify.
3. To displease.

Consumiçám [kọnsumi'saŋ] *n*
1. Consumption.
2. Displeasure.
3. Tease.

Consumido [kọnsu'midu] *adj*
1. Displeased.
2. Quarrelsome.

Conventona [koŋven'tọna] *n*
Girl, usually orphaned, brought up in a convent.

Copa [‘kǫpa] *n*
Sideboard.

Copám [kǫ’paŋ] *n*
A large glass.

Copito [kǫ’pitu] *n*
A small glass.

Côpo-côpo [‘kọpo ‘kọpo] *n* (<*M. kupu-kupu*)
Butterfly.

Coquéra [kǫ’kęra] *n*
Coconut cake filled with dessicated coconut, eggs and sugar.

Coquéta [ko’kęta] *adj*
Coquette, who likes to engage the attention of men.

Coquinho [kọ’kiɲo] *n*
Water chestnut, *Scirpus tuberosus*.

Coraçám [kǫra’saŋ]*n*
Heart. *Êle sâm bôm-coraçám é* he is a kind-hearted person. ***Bôm coraçám*** [bọŋ kǫra’saŋ] kind-hearted, generous person.
❖ ***Coraçám cósca*** [kǫra’saŋ ‘kǫska] someone who wants to speak out but remains quiet. See **Cósca**.
❖ ***Coraçám duro*** [kǫra’saŋ ‘duru] dispassionate, cruel.
❖ ***Coraçám grándi*** [kǫra’saŋ ‘grandi] generous.
❖ ***Coraçám móli*** [kǫra’saŋ ‘mǫli] soft-hearted.
❖ ***Coraçám tánto*** [kǫra’saŋ ‘tąntu] talkative person.
Mau coraçám [mąw kǫra’saŋ] unkind person.

Corázi [kǫ’rązi] *n*
Courage.

Cordial [kurdi’ąl] *n* (<*Eng. cordial*)
1. Remedy in the form of a powder scraped from a calcareous stone of Indian origin, which was formerly used to calm nerves.
2. Fruit cordial.

Corê [kǫ'rẹ] *vi*

To run.

❖***Corê greza*** [kǫ'rẹ 'grẹza] to go to church on Maundy Thursday.

Corê trás [kǫ'rẹ trąs] to follow.

Corê vai [kǫ'rẹ vại] to run along.

Corê vai, corê vêm [kǫ'rẹ vại kǫ'rẹ vẹŋ] to come and go in a hurry.

Corenteza [kǫren'tẹza] *n*

1. Breeze.

2. Flow of air created by opening two windows or doors in a house.

Sentâ na corenteza, pôde ficâ doente sitting in a draught can make you feel unwell.

Corn-star [kọn'stą] *n* (<*Eng. corn starch*)

Cake made with corn starch, hence the name. Also called **genete**.

Corta-Corta [kǫrta'kǫrta] *n*

Kite competition to try to cut an opponent's string. See **Sarangông**.

Corta-vento ['kǫrta 'vẹntu] *n*

Somebody with an aquiline nose.

Corte ['kǫrte] *n* (<*Eng. court*)

Court.

Cósca ['kǫska] *n*

Tickles.

❖ ***Coraçám-cosca*** [kǫra'saŋ 'kǫska] somebody who wants to speak out but remains quiet.

Coscorám [kusku'raŋ] *n*

Typical Christmas sweetmeat, made with flour, eggs and molasses, and dusted with sugar.

Cosquénta [kǫs'kẹnta] *adj*

Tickly.

Costa ['kǫsta] *n*

Back.

❖ ***Atirâ na costa!*** [ąti'rą na 'kǫsta] don't pay any

attention; leave it alone; don't bother about it!

❖*Costa-quênti* [ʻkǫsta ʼkẹnti] defender, person in a high position who protects those under him.

Costumado [kostuʼmąduj] *adj*
Used to, accustomed. *Êle costumado vêm cedo* he usually comes early. *Nunca costumado têm chuva Otubro* it's unusual to have rain in October.

Costurâ [kǫstuʼrạ] *vi & vt*
To sew.

Cote [ʻkǫte] *n*
1. Twist, sprain.
2. Cracking of bones.

Cotê [kǫʼtẹ] *adj & adv*
Tottering, stumbling. *Andâ cotê-cotê* to limp, hobble.

Côto [ʻkọto] *n*
1. Knuckle.
2. Elbow.
3. Any hard object that protrudes, for instance the handle of a walking stick. *Côto di nariz* protruding part of nose.

Cou-iok [koʼiọk] *n* (<*C. ieok*[2] *kou*[3] 藥膏)
Chinese medicinal paste.

Cóvado [ʻkọvadọ] *n*
Chinese measurement of length, approximately 38 cm. Also called **pau**.

Côve-côco [ʻkọvi ʻkọku] *n*
Cabbage (*Brassica oleracea*).

Cozinhâ [koziʼɲạ] *vt*
To cook.

Crê [ʻkrẹ] *vt*
To believe. *Iou nádi crê* I won't believe it.

Crecê [krẹʼsẹ] *vi*
To grow.

Crecedura [krẹsẹʼdurạ] *n*
Growth.

Crecido [kre'sidu] See **Quecido**.

Crioula [kri'ọlạ] *n*
Orphaned girl, formerly taken into a family home where her status would fall in-between that of a daughter and that of a maid.

Cristám [kris'taŋ] *n*
Catholic.
Cristám-nôvo [kris'taŋ 'nọvo] adult Chinese convert.
Língu cristám ['liŋgu kris'taŋ] Portuguese or patois.
Papiâ cristám [pa'pyạkris'taŋ] to speak Portuguese or patois.

Cú [ku] *n*
Backside, behind.
❖***Cú tremido*** [ku tre'midu] afraid.
❖***Nôm têm mama, nôm têm cú*** [nọŋ tẹŋ 'mạma nọŋ tẹŋ ku] flat-chested, flat-bottomed.
See **Pobre**, ***Pobre-cú-limpado***.

Cuçâ [ku'sạ] *vt*
To scratch.
❖***Cuçâ cabeça*** [ku'sạ ka'bẹsa] to be at a loss.
See **Sarna,** ***Sarna pa cuçâ***.

Cucêra [ku'sẹra] *n*
Scratch, rash.

Cucús [ku'kuš], **cuscús** [kuš'kuš] *adj*
Steamed.

Cudí [ku'di] *vt*
To assist, help. *Gente, cudí, cudí pa iou!* help, somebody!

Cudum [ku'duŋ] *adj* (*<M. kudong*)
Short in stature.

Culau [ku'lạu], **colau** [kọ'lạu] *n* (*<C. kou*[1] *lau*[4] 歌樓)
Chinese restaurant. *Chacha co Avo-công tudo dia pramicêdo têm na culau* grandmother and grandfather are at the Chinese restaurant every day.

Cúli ['kuli] *n*
1. Coolie, rickshaw or trishaw coolie. *Chomâ quanto cúli-cúli para cartâ tudo ancuza* to

hire some coolies to carry everything.
2. Useless, person of no worth.

Cumpridám [kumpri'daŋ] *adj*
Very long.

Cumungâ [kumuŋ'gạ] *vi*
To confess.

Cumunhám [kumuŋaŋ] *n*
Communion.

Cunfissâ [kuɱfi'sạ] *vt*
To confess.

Curto-curto ['kurtọ 'kurtọ] *adj*
Very short.

Curum [ku'ruŋ] *n* (<*M. kurong*)
Cage, chicken run. *Curum di galinha* hen house.

Cuscús [kuš'kuš] See **cucús**.

Cuspidô [kuspi'dọ] *n*
Spittoon.

Custâ [kus'tạ] *vi*
1. To cost.
2. To require effort, be difficult.

Cutám [ku'taŋ] *n* (<*M. kutang*)
Bodice. *Saia-cutám* woman's combinations, made of skirt and bodice.

Cute ['kuti] See **cutí**.

Cutí [ku'ti], **cute** ['kuti] *n & vt* (<*M. kutil*)
1. Blow to the head.
2. To hit someone with any object.

Cutí piám [ku'ti pi'aŋ] *n*
1. Spinning top game.
2. The top used for this game, also called **piám carreta**.

Cuza ['kuza] *adv*
What? Which? Contraction of *Quê cuza?*
Cuza chomâ iou tai-mong? why are you calling me stupid? *Cuza fazê churá?* why are you crying? *Cuza fazê churâ?* what's the point of crying?

Cuza vôs querê? what do you want? *Cuza vôs tâ papiá?* what are you saying? *Quê cuza pôde fazê?* what can be done? *Quê cuza?* what was that?

Cuza suzo [kuza'suzu] *n*

1. Filthy thing.
2. Vulgar thing.
3. Damned thing.
4. Spirit, ghost.

Dâ [dạ] *vt*
To give.
Dâ cara [dạ 'kạ·ra] to pay attention to.
Dâ cavaco [dạ kạ'vạku] to take offence.
Dâ comê [dạ kọ'mẹ] to feed. *Dâ comê gente* to supply food, accept orders for food.
Dâ co falta [dạ ku 'fạlta] to notice the lack.
Dâ co queixo [dạ ku 'keišu] to expire.
Dâ côr di si [dạ kọr di'si] to give news.
Dâ côti [dạ 'kọti] to have a cramp, twist.
Dâ fundo [dạ 'fundu] to stop.
Dâ vestí [dạ vis'ti] to help dress.
Dâ lembrança [dạ lẹm'brạnsa] to send regards to.
Dâ mordecim [dạ mọrdi'siŋ] to annoy.

Dachim [da'čiŋ] *n* (<*C. toh⁴ tsing³* 砣秤)
See **Ta-chim**.

Daia ['dạia] *n*
Midwife.

Daiôm [dại'ọŋ] *n* (<*M. dayong*)
Large wooden spatula shaped like an oar, used for preparing **alúa**, guava jam, dodol, and other Macanese jams.

Dále ['dạli] *vt*
1. To attack, beat, smack. *Pegâ dále* to give a hiding. *Pegâ vassôra-pena dále quiança* to beat a child with a feather duster.
2. To imbibe; to enjoy imbibing. *Dále vinho* to drink wine. *Dále grog* to take alcohol.
3. To gamble. ***Nôs tâ vai dále dos mám*** [nọs ta vai dạ'li dọs maŋ] we're going to have a flutter.
❖ ***Dále dôs mám co inglês*** [dạ'li dọs maŋ ku iŋ'glẹs] said when the father is unknown.

Damostrâ [damọs'trạ] *vt* (<*P. dar + mostrar*)

1. To show.
2. To demonstrate.

Dangeroso [daɲǰe'rọzo] *adj* (<*Eng. dangerous*)
1. Risky.
2. Dangerous.

Daretê [dare'tẹ] *vi & vt*
1. To melt.
2. To fall in love.

Daretido [dare'tidu] *adj*
1. Melted.
2. Slobbery.

Deco ['dẹku] See **Ôlo deco**.

Dedo ['dẹdu] *n*
Finger. Toe.
Dedo-côm ['dẹdu kọŋ] thumb.

Defronte [de'frọnti] *n*
Damned soul.
Uví, defronte! listen, dammit!

Dengue-dengue ['deŋgi 'deŋgi], **dingo-dingo** ['diŋgu·'diŋgu] *adj*
Floppy, slack, not secure. *Porta dingo-dingo* flimsy door.

Dente ['dẹnti] *n*
Tooth, teeth. *Gossô dente* to brush one's teeth.
Dente ricusâ ['dẹnti riku'zạ] my teeth can't take (chew) it. As tough as leather.

Derdezido [derde'zidu] *adv*
Intentionally. *Iou derdezido vêm olâ vôs* I've come to see you on purpose.

Deusalembrâ [dewzalem'brạ] See **Diosalembrâ**.

Despique [des'piki] *n*
Quarrel, argument.

Dessâ [dẹ'sạ] *vt*
To leave. *Dessâ iou olâ* let me see. *Nê-bôm dessâ véla cai* don't let the old lady fall.
Dessâ vai-ia! [dẹ'sạ 'vại ya] let it be!, ignore it!

Destung'a [des'tuŋa] See **Estung'a**.

Devoçám [devọ'saŋ] *n*
Devotion.

Di [di] *prep*
Of. Indicates the semantic relation between two elements: such as possession, origin, place, commonly used with interjections. *Uí di bôm!* Very good. *Êle pôssa di grándi* he is very big!

Diabo ['dyạbu] *n*
1. Devil.
Diabo dâ capa, diabo dâ campenha ['dyạbu dạ 'kạpa 'dyạbu dạ kam'pẹɲa] If the devil gives you a cloak, he will also give you a bell, in other words a criminal will always leave clues behind.
Diabo-solto ['dyạbu 'soltu] Bedevilled.
2. Spirit, ghost, soul from the afterworld.
3. Heavy Macanese dish prepared with leftovers flavoured with various condiments such as Chinese mustard.

Diabo-cacinha ['dyạbu ka'siɲa] *adj*
1. Evil.
2. Provocative.

Dicotado [dikọ'tạdu] *adj*
1. Low cut (garment).
2. Low cut. *Nhônha dicotado* woman who wears revealing clothes.

Di-frónti [di'frọnti] *adv*
Ahead, in front.

Dingo-dingo ['diŋgu·'diŋgu] See **dengue-dengue**.

Dios [di'ọs] *n*
God. *Dios dâ graça* God be with you. *Dios sabe* God knows. *Dios haja* (used of one who has died) with God.

Diosalembrâ [dioẓalem'brạ], **deusalembrâ** [dewzalem'brạ] *adj & n*
Deceased. *syn* **Diosaja**.

Diosaja [diọs'ạǰa] *n*
With God. Used of deceased relative or close friend. *Iou-sa diosaja* my deceased husband/wife.

Diospiro di água [di'ọspirọ di 'ạgwa] *n*
Persimmon (*Dyospiros kaki*), reddish-orange fruit shaped like a tomato, with hard flesh. See **figo cáqui**.

Disbocado [disbọ'kạdu] *n*
Person who uses obscene language.

Discarado [diska'rạdu] *adj*
1. Shamed, without honour. *Ai, iou qui discarado, azinha iscondê, non quêro olâ!* I was so ashamed that I hid and could not bear to look any more!
2. Shameless.

Discarso [dis'kạrsu] *adj*
Barefoot.

Discompô [diskọm'pọ] *vi*
To give a telling off.

Disintôm[1] [dizin'tọŋ] *adj*
Out of tune.

Disintôm[2] [dizin'tọŋ] *vi*
To sing off key.

Dismanchâ [dismɲ'čạ] *vi & vt*
1. To abort.
2. To dismantle, demolish. *China tâ dismanchâ baraca* the Chinese are taking down the scaffolding. *Casa dismanchado* demolished house.

Dismancho [dis'mɲču] *n*
1. Abortion.
Ung'a dismancho trás di ôtro a series of abortions.
2. Hindrance. *Êle sâm ung'a dismancho-prazer* he is a killjoy.

Disparecê [disparẹ'sẹ] *vi*
To disappear. *Vosôtro já disparecê qui cedo* you disappeared early on.

Divera [di'vera] *adv*
1. Really. *Maria divera bunita* Maria is really pretty.
2. Truth. *Sâm divera* it's the truth.

Divinhâ [divi'ɲạ] *vt*
To guess.

Divinhaçám [diviɲa'saŋ] *n*
1. Prophecy.
2. Riddle.

Dizaforado [dizafo'rạdu] *adj*
1. Daring.
2. Crude.

Dizafôro [diza'fọro] *n*
Daring, abuse. *Qui dizaforo!* how dare he! *Seléa dizaforo* similar abuse.

Dizavegonhado [dizavego'ɲạdu] *adj*
Shameless, blatant. *Acung'a dizavegonhado* that shameless person.

Dizémbro [di'zẹmbru] *n*
December.

Dizencantâ [dizeŋkan'tạ] *vt*
To reveal, to find. *Úndi já vai dizencantâ estung'a chapeu* where did you find that hat? *Quelê-môdo já dizencantâ noiva assí chistosa* how did you find such a lovely bride?

Dizengonçado [dizeŋgon'sạdu] *adj*
1. Clumsy.
2. Accident-prone.

Dizuvido [dizu'bidu] *adj*
Disobedient.

Dó [dọ], **dol** [dọl] *n*
Black veil worn by elderly women when attending church. *Nôs véla-véla têm-qui cubrí dol pa vai greza* nós, we old ladies have to cover our heads with a **dol** when we go to church.

Dóci [‘dǫsi] *n*
Sweet.
Dóci camalénga [‘dǫsi kama’lęŋga] pumpkin jam.
Dóci-dóci [‘dǫsi ‘dǫsi] sweetened.
Dóci vestido [‘dǫsi vis’tidu] selection of decorated sweets given to the guests at a christening or wedding.

Doda [‘dǫda] See **Dôdo**.

Dôdo [‘dọdu] *adj m,* **doda** [‘dọda] *adj f*
Crazy.

Dodol [dọ’dǫl] *n* (*<M. kueh dodol*)
Dessert made with pear jam, pine nuts, brown sugar, coconut, almonds, butter, lard and glutinous rice.

Dói [dọi] *vi & n*
1. To hurt. *Dói únde?* where does it hurt?
2. Ache. *Dói boca* toothache. *Dói cabeça* headache. *Dói bariga* stomach ache. *Dói uvido* earache.

Dol [dǫl] See **Dó**.

Dôs [dọs] *num*
Two. *Isquevê dós regra pa iou* drop me a couple of lines.

Dozelado [dọze’lądu] *adj*
Kneeling.

Drento [‘drẹntu] *adv*
Within, inside.

Drêto [‘drẹtu] *adj*
Right, just. *Sâm drêto* it’s fair. *Bêm di drêto* very accurate.

Durmí [dur’mi] *vi*
To sleep.

Durmido [dur’midu] *adj & vi*
To be sleeping. *Já ficâ durmido* he fell asleep.

Drumí [dru’mi] *vi*
See **Durmí**.

Égu [‘ęgu] *n*
Mare.

Elâ [ę’la] *vt* (<*M. helak*)
1. To pull.
2. To drag. *Elâ na rabicho di quiada* to pull a child’s plait.

Êle [’eli] *pro*
He, she.

Êle-sa [‘eli sa] See **Êle-sua**.

Êle-sua [‘eli ‘sua], **êle-sa** [‘eli sa] *adj*
His, her. See **Sa**.

Emâ [ę’mạ] *vi* (<*P. ema*)
1. To eat like a glutton, stuff oneself.
2. To eat sweetmeats.

Emado [ę’madu] *adj*
Glutton, sweet tooth.

Embarcaçám [embarka’saŋ] *n*
Generic word for a Chinese fishing or boat, formerly with sails and nowadays with an engine.

Embrulâ [embru’la] *vt*
1. To pack.
2. To wrap.

Empada [ẹm’pạda] See **Impada**.

Empatucâ [impatu’kạ] *vt*
To open one’s eyes wide, goggle.
Ôlo empatucado [‘ọlu impatu’kądu] pop-eyed. *Qui têm goita, pôde têm ôlo empatucado* people with goitre may develop puffy eyes.

Empê [em’pẹ] **impê** [im’pẹ] *vi*
To stand.

Empido [em’pidu] **impido** [im’pidu] *adv*
On your feet.

Empolado [empo’lądu] *adj*
Extruding.

Encapelâ [enkąpe’la] *vt*
1. To wrap oneself in a cape.
2. To wrap up. *Já encapelâ qui tánto rópa* he dressed warmly.

Êncha [‘ẹɲča], **enchóna** [‘eɲ’čọna] *adj*
Impolite, tasteless. *Ela qui encha! Usâ rópa cumprido pindurado!* she has such bad taste! Her clothes were so ill-fitting.

Enchê [‘ẹɲ’čẹ] See **inchí**.

Enchido [ẹɲ’čidu] See **Inchido**.

Enchóna [‘eɲ’čọna] See **Êncha**.

Encorpado [eŋkor’pądu] *adj*
1. Fat, thick. *Sópa encorpado* rich, heavy soup.
2. Sturdy. *Árvre qui encorpado* a solid, well-developed tree.

Encunhâ [eŋku’ɲạ] *vt*
1. To prop up.
2. To lean. *Ieu já encunhâ êle na parede* I leant it against the wall.
3. To get into a fix.

É-né? [ẹ ’nẹ], **né?** [nẹ] *interrog*
Isn’t that right? *syn* **Sâm nunca**.

Enfadâ [ẹɱfa’dạ] *vi & vt*
1. To cast a spell.
2. To irk. *Nê-bôm enfadâ gente co vosso papiaçám* don’t bother people with your chattering.

Enfadado [ẹɱfą’dądu] *adj*
Irked, peeved. *Iou já uví qui ficâ enfadado* I was riled just hearing about it.

Enfeâ [eɱfe’a] *vt*
1. To make ugly.
2. To bring dishonour. *Enfeâ nomi di pai-mai* he brought his parents’ name into disrepute.

Enfeado [eɱfe’adu] *adj*
1. Disgraced.
2. Infamous.

Enfetiçâ [eɱfeti’sạ] *vt*
1. To bewitch. See also **Bagatiâ**.
2. To seduce.

Enfêtiçado [eɱfẹti’sadu] *adj*
1. Bewitched. See also **Bagatiado**.

2. Seduced.

Engajamento [eŋgaǰa'mẹnto] *n* (<*Eng. engagement*).
Engagement.

Engajâ [eŋga'ǰạ] *vt*
To ask a father for his daughter's hand in marriage.

Engalinhâ [eŋgạli'ɲạ] *vt*
To bring bad luck, make unlucky.

Entafulâ [entafu'la], **tafulâ** [tafu'la] *vt*
To stuff one's mouth or stomach with food, glut.

Entena [en'tẹna] *n*
Roof beam, used in old houses in Macao.

Entiçâ [enti'sạ] *vt* (<*Eng. entice*)
1. To tempt.
2. To incite, urge.

Entornâ [entor'nạ] *vt*
1. To spill.
2. To flow over.

Entrestanto [entres'tạntu] *adv & conj*
Meanwhile, in the meantime.

Entretê [entre'tẹ] *vt*
To entertain. *Entretê onçóm* to keep oneself amused.

Envegonhâ [eɱvergo'ɲạ] *vt*
1. To shame.
2. To cast a shadow. *Envegonhâ naçám* to be a national disgrace.

Erguí [er'gi] *vt*
1. To raise, lift. *Erguí casa* to build a house.
2. To get up. *Erguí di cama* to get out of bed.
3. To suspend.

Escabelâ [skạbe'lạ] *vt*
To hurt.
Pegâ escabelâ to pull somebody's hair.

Escarchada [eskar'šạda] *n*
Embroidery made with silver

or gold thread in relief, and sometimes decorated with sequins.

Escurecê [skure'sẹ] *vi*

To turn into night. *Cavâ escurecê* after dusk.

Esfolâ [esfo'lạ] *vi & vt*

1. To fleece.
2. To spend.
3. To break another person's bank.

Esfregâ [sfrę'gạ] *vt*

To scrub clean. *Esfregâ chám* to scrub the floor.

Esgrabulâ [sgrabu'lạ] *vt*

1. To tousle the hair, get one's hair in a mess.
2. To turn upside down, dismantle.

Esguichâ [sgi'čạ] *vt*

1. To gush.
2. To throw out.
3. To push out.

❖ ***Têm qui esguichâ sapeca*** [tẹŋ ki sgi'čạ sa'pęka] it's time to pay.

Esmolâ [ezmo'lạ] *vi*

1. To live on alms.
2. To be as poor as a churchmouse. *Têm qui esmolâ pa nádi morê di fome* he has to beg in order not to starve to death.

Espevitâ [espevitạ] *vt*

1. To behave in an affected manner.
2. To spread.

Espevitado[1] [espevi'tadu] *adj*

Pretentious.

Espevitado[2] [espevi'tadu] *n*

Know-all. Person who shows off his knowledge.

Espigado [spi'gạdu] *adj*

Grown, much taller. *Ai! qui grándi já ficâ estung'a quiança, qui espigado!* this child has really grown, he's so tall!

Espinhela [spi'ɲęla] *n*
Spine.

Espitún [spi'tun] *n* (<*Eng. spittoon*)
Spittoon.

Estendê [sten'dẹ] *vt*
1. To stretch.
2. To extend. *Estendê na chám* to stretch out on the ground.
❖ ***Estendê língu*** [sten'dẹ 'liŋgu] to speak ill of people.

Estirâ [sti'rạ] *vi*
To stretch out. *Estirado na chám* stretched out on the ground.

Estômo [s'tọmo] *n*
Stomach.

Estonteâ [stonte'ạ] *vt*
To stun.

Estopôr [sto'pọr] *n*
1. Ugly person.
2. Bad person.
3. Good-for-nothing. *Êle qui estopôr* he's so useless.

Estoporâ [estapọ'rạ] *vt*
To curse.

Estória [es'tọria] *n*
1. History.
2. Story, anecdote. *Úndi vôs uví estung'a estória?* where did you hear that?
❖ ***Tánto estória!*** ['tąntu s'tọria] so much to talk about and it's all lies!

Estravagáncia [estrava'gąnsia] *n*
1. Extravagance. *Fazê estravagáncia* to indulge.
2. Luxury. *Vivo na estravagáncia* to live in style.

Estrica [s'trika], **istrica** [is'trika] *n* (<*D. strijke*)
Iron (domestic).

Estricâ [stri'ka], **istricâ** [istri'ka] *vt* (<*D. strijke*)
To iron. *Estricâ rópa* to iron clothes.

Estung'a [es'tuŋa] *dem*

This. *Estung'a quanto* these. *Estung'a quanto casa sâm bem di feo* these houses are horrible. *Estung'a ancusa* this.

Destung'a [des'tuŋa] (<*Maq. di + estung'a*)

That. *Destung'a manêra* that way.

Estúrdia [s'turdia] *n*

1. Prank, recklessness. *Êle sâm ung'a estúrdia* he's a wag.

2. Folly. *Já fazê estúrdia* he played a joke.

Ezazerâ [ezazę'rạ] *vi*

To exaggerate.

Façám [fą'saŋ] *n* (<*C. fa*^{1} *sang*^{1} 花生)
Peanut.

Faca-garfo ['fąka 'gąrfu], *n*
Cutlery. *syn* **Colê-garfo**.

Facarám [faka'raŋ] *n*
Large knife.

Faceta [fą'sẹta] *n*
1. Dressy woman.
2. Vain woman.

Fáci ['fąsi] *adj*
Easy. *Fáci qui fáci* very easy.

Fa-hóc [fą'họk] *adj* (<*C. fa*^{3} *hok*^{6} 化學)
Weak, feeble, unresisting. *Sobrado fa-hóc* weak floor.

Faichi [fąi'či] *n* (<*C. fai*^{3} *chi*^{2} 筷子)
Chopsticks.

Faichista [fąi'čista] *n* (<*C. fai*^{3} *chi*^{2} 筷子 + *P. -ista*)
Man who plays <fan-tan>, removing groups of four counters (formerly **sapecas**) with a rod, to get the final result. The rod is a form of long **faichi**.

Faifum [fai'fuŋ] *n* (<*C. fai*^{3} *fong*^{1} 快風)
1. Illness with similar symptoms to malaria.
2. Flatulence.

Faitiám [fąti'aŋ] *n* (<*C. fai*^{3} *teang*^{2} 快艇)
Light, speedy Chinese boat used for transporting goods and people.

Faizám [fai'zaŋ] *n*
Pheasant.

Falâ [fą'lą] *vt*
1. To speak.
2. To say. *Iou virâ falâ co êle* I turned to him, saying. *Iou uví falâ* I heard tell.
Falâ divera [fą'lą di'vęra] tell the truth.
Falâ mánso-mánso [fą'lą 'mąnsu 'mąnsu] to speak in a soft voice.

Falâ vai, falâ vêm [fą'lą vai fą'lą vęŋ] to say and repeat.
Falâ portuguezado [fą'lą portuge'zą du] to use Portuguese expressions or accent when speaking.
Falâ sâm-ia [fą'lą saŋ ya] to agree reluctantly.

Faladéra [fala'dęra] *n*
Tittle-tattler.

Falânpám [fąlaŋ'paŋ] *n* (<*Eng. frying pan*)
Frying pan.

Falhâ [fą'λą] *vi & vt*
To fail.
Falhâ mám to fail to grasp well, letting slip an object.

Fan-tan [fąn'tąn] *n* (<*C. fan*[1] *tan*[1] 番攤)
Chinese gambling game which consists of guessing the number of remaining counters from a pile hidden under an upturned cup, after as many groups of four as possible have been removed. See **Faichista**.

Fantanéro [fąntą'nęro] *n* (<*C. fan*[1] *tan*[1] 番攤 + *P. -ero*)
Fan-tan addict.

Faquiâ [fąki'ą] *vt*
To stab.

Fantuchêro [fąntu'čero] *adj & n*
1. Exaggerated, far-fetched.
2. Fantasist.
3. Amazing.
4. Chatterbox, blatherskite.

Farinha-pau [fą'riɲa pąw] *n*
Sago flour.

Fárti ['fąrti] *n*
Sweetmeat made at Christmastime with flour, coconut, pine nuts, almonds and spices. Also called <**Almofada do menino Jesus**>.

Fastio [fas'tiu] *n*
1. Boredom.

2. Aversion.
3. Laziness.

Fata-fata [‘fąta ’fąta], **feti-feti** [‘fęti ’fęti] *adj*
Unscrewed, insane. *syn* **Tóc-tóc**.

Favôr [fą’vọ] *n*
Favour. *Fazê favô* please.

Fazê [fa’zę] *vt*
1. To make.
2. To achieve.
Fazê floristia [fa’zę flores’tia] (i) to show off; (ii) to spend ostentatiously.
Fazê galantaria [fa’zę galanta’ria] to flirt, court.
Fazê tentaçám [fa’zę tenta’saŋ] to tempt, seduce.
Fazê vista [fa’zę ‘vista] to look good.
Fazê susto [fa’zę ‘sustu] to scare.

Fazénda [fa’zęnda] *n*
Cloth.

Fêde[1] [‘fęde] *adj*
Stinky.
Bôca fêde [‘bọka ‘fęde] bad breath, halitosis.

Fêde[2] [‘fęde] *vi*
To give off body odor, or a foul smell. *Fêde mizinha* stinking of medicine. *Fêde catiaca* or *Fêde raposo* stinking of sweat. See also **Impestâ**.
❖***Tâ fêde-ia*** [tą ‘fęde ya] she’s pregnant now.

Fedorento [fędo’ręntu] *adj*
1. Unpleasant.
2. Undesirable.

Feióna [fei’ọna] *adj*
Very ugly.

Fêmea [‘fęmia] *adj & n*
Female.

Fendê [fen’dę] *vt*
1. To cleave open, fissure.
2. To split. *Fendê linha* to chop wood.

Feo [‘fęu] *adj*
Ugly.
Feo olâ [‘fęu o’lạ] it doesn’t suit you.

Ferâ [fę’rạ] *vt*
1. To deceive *Nê-bôm ferâ iou* don’t trick me.
2. To trick.
Ferâ cám [fę’rạ kaŋ] to swindle.
Ferâ lampâna [fę’rạ lạm’pạna] to dupe.
3. To fry. *Ferâ na tacho* to cook in a frying pan.

Ferado [fę’rạdu] *adj*
1. Swindled.
2. Duped.

Fervido [fer’vidu] *adj*
Boiled. Boiling, very hot.

Festa [‘fęsta] *n*
Party.
Festa di quebrâ testa [‘fęsta di kę’bra ’tęsta] (i) Ball. (ii) Solemn event, commemoration.
Festa di fichâ ano [‘fęsta di fi’čạ ‘anu] party marking an anniversary.
Missa festa [‘misa ‘fęsta] high mass.

Feti-feti [fęti-fęti] *adj*
See **Fata-fata**.

Fêto [‘fęto] *adj*
Done.

Feveréro [fęvę’ręro] *n*
February.

Fevôr [fę’vọ] *n*
1. Fervour.
2. Devotion.

Fiâ [fi’ạ] *vi & vt*
1. To warrant.
2. To buy or sell on tick.

Ficâ [fi’kạ] *vi*
1. To remain, become, change into.
❖***Ficâ daretido*** [fi’kạ dare’tidu] to become excessively excited.

2. To be located.
3. To reside. *Ficâ na Macau* to live in Macao.

Fichâ [fi'čạ] *vt*
To close.
Fichâ ano [fi'čạ 'anu] to have a birthday.
Fichâ ôlo [fi'čạ 'ọlu] (i) to close one's eyes; (ii) to die.

Fifó [fi'fǫ] *part*
Onomatopaeic term used only in the expression **fifó-churâ** to weep inconsolably. *Qui-pôde, tudo ora fifó-churâ* she's a tragedy queen, weeping inconsolably all the time.

Figo ['figu] *n*
1. Banana.
Figo-chêroso ['figu če'rọso] banana, with yellow peel dotted with brown.
Figo-horta ['figu 'ǫrta] variety of banana called <*sai*[1] *ieong*[4] *chiu*[1] 西洋蕉>, in Chinese, with a smooth yellow skin and astringent flesh, shorter and fatter than **figo-chêroso**.
Figo-vilám ['figu vi'laŋ] small, inferior quality banana, also called *coolie banana*.
2. General name for other fruits.
Figo-capote ['figu kạ'pǫti] sapota, (*Manilkora zapota*).
Figo-cáqui ['figu 'kạki] kaki.
3. Fig, ***figo di Portugal*** ['figu di pọrtu'gạl].

Figuêra [fi'gẹra] *n*
1. Banana palm.
2. Fig tree.

Figurino [figu'rinọ] *n*
Fashion magazine.

Fijám [fi'ǰaŋ] *n*
Bean.
Fijám-vemêlo [fi'ǰaŋ vẹ'mẹlọ] bean used for bean stew.
Fijám-frade [fi'ǰaŋ 'frạdi] black-eyed bean.
Fijám-chicote [fi'ǰaŋ či'kǫti] kind of Chinese runner bean. See also **Tacó**.

Filâ [fi'lạ] *vt*

1. To clutch.
2. To grab.

Filiz [fi'lis] *adj*

Happy. *Tâ vivo filiz* he is very happy.

Fila ['filạ] *n*

Daughter. *Fila-fila* daughters.

Filo[1] ['filu] *adj*

Small, diminutive.

See **Chuva, *Chuva filo-filo***.

Filo[2] ['filu] *n*

Child. *Filo-filo* sons, children.

Filo-di-quim ['filu di kiŋ] *Lit.* whose son.

❖***Filo-di-hui*** ['filu di wi] each of the members of a **hui**. See **Hui**.

Filo-grándi ['filu 'grandi] oldest child.

❖ ***Filo trás di porta*** ['filu trạs di 'portạ] or ***trás di Lapa*** ['filu trạs di 'lạpa] illegitimate child.

Finâ [fi'nạ] *vi*

To expire, die.

Fineza [fi'nęza] *n*

1. Refinement.
2. Kindness.

Fingí [fiɲ'ǰi] See **Finzí**.

Fingido [fiɲ'ǰidu] *adj*

Hypocrite.

Fino ['finu] *adj*

1. Narrow. *Fino cumprido* long and narrow.
2. Thin. *Fino-fino* very thin, in small pieces. *Boca fino-fino* to be inaudible.

Finório [fi'nǫriu] *adj*

Somebody who takes offence easily.

Finura [fi'nura] *n*

Fineness.

Finzí [fin'zi], **fingí** [fiɲ'ǰi] *vi*

To pretend. *Finzí tolo*, pretend to be stupid. *Finzí triste* to pretend to be sad.

See **Alonço, *finzí alonço***.

Fio [fiw] *n*

String, thread.

Fio-mézinha ['fiw mę'ziɲa] string used for paper kites or **sarangôm**, specially made with glue and ground glass for games of **corta-corta** or **cortâ papagaio**.

Firaco [fi'rąku] *n*

Abandoned child.

Fita ['fita] *n*

1. Tape. Narrow strip of cloth used for decoration, or as a link.

Fita di sapato ['fita di sa'pątu] shoelaces.

2. Strip.

Fita-cinéma ['fita si'nęma] film.

❖ ***Fazê-fita*** [fa'zę 'fita] duplicitous.

❖ ***Olâ fita*** [ǫ'lą 'fita] to go to cinema.

Fitéro [fi'tęro] *n*

Cranky person, insincere person.

Fléma ['flęma] *n*

Phlegm.

Floristia [floris'tia] *n*

1. Game.

2. Extravagance.

Floristriâ [florestri'ą] *vi*

To play, amuse oneself.

Fluquêro [flu'kęro] *n* (<*Eng. fluke*)

Lucky person.

Fluquice [flu'kisi] *n*

1. Good luck at gambling.

2. Successful game, by chance, a stroke of luck. *Qui fluquice!* lucky!

3. Casual success in any endeavour.

Fo-chai [fǫ'čąi] *n* (<*C. fo² chai⁴* 火柴)

Matches.

Fôfo ['fǫfo] *adj*

Soft.

Fogám [fọ'gaŋ] *n*
1. Oven.
2. Hearth.

Fola [fǫla] See **Fólia**.

Fólia ['fǫlia], **fola** ['fǫla] *n*
1. Leaf.
Fola di olado ['fǫla di o'lądọ] leaf of a medicinal plant used to counter the evil eye.
2. Page.
3. Newspaper. *Já sai na fólia* it was published in the newspaper.

Fómi ['fǫmi] *adj & n*
1. Starving.
2. Hunger.

Fonçám [fọŋ'saŋ] *n*
Party. *Assistí fonçám* to go to a party.

Fontám [fọn'taŋ] *n*
Small pantry cupboard with net doors for storing food and condiments.

Fónti ['fǫnti] *n*
Fountain, well.
Agu-fónti ['agu 'fǫnti] fresh water from the well.

Fóquei ['fǫkẹi], [fǫ'kại] See **Foquí**.

Foquí [fǫ'ki], **fóquei** [fǫ'kẹi], [fǫ'kại] *n* (<*C. fo*[2] *kei*[3] 伙記)
Chinese waiter.
See also **Bói**.

Fora ['fǫra] *adv*
1. Outside; exterior.
Gente-fora ['ǰẹnti 'fǫra] people outside the family.
2. More than, so many. *Um cento fora* a hundred odd.

Franzí [fran'zi] *vt*
To frown. *Franzí testa* to frown in anger.

Frenético [frẹ'nẹtiku] *adj*
1. Impatient.
2. Neurotic.

Frescura [frẹs'kura] *n*
Lemonade or other summer

drink. *Bebê frescura* to drink something cool.

Frialdade [friąl'dądi] *n*
Coolness.

Friza ['friza] *n* (<*Eng. freezer*)
Freezer.

Frónha ['frǫɲa] *n*
1. Cover.
2. Middle-aged woman. *Olâ seléa fronha* to see a similar kind of woman (as one in her forties).

Fruta-manila ['fruta ma'nila] *n*
Almond. *syn* **Façám**.

Fruta-rosa [fruta'rǫza] *n*
syn **Jambo**.

Frutázi [fru'tązi] *n*
Selection of fruits.

Fucinhâ [fu'siɲạ] *vi*
To imitate an animal's snout. To indicate displeasure.

Fucinho [fu'siɲu] *n*
Snout. *Fazê fucinho porco* to imitate a pig's snout.

Fugâ [fu'gạ] *vi*
1. To suffocate with any liquid or foodstuff.
2. To drown.
3. To sauté.

Fugí [fu'ǰi] See **Fuzí**.

Fula ['fula] *n*
1. Flower. *Fula-fula* flowers.
Fula-coco ['fula 'kǫku] magnolia blossom (*Magnolia pumila* or *Liriodendron coco*).
Fula-figo ['fula 'figu] fragrant, banana-scented creamy-white magnolia blossom (*Liriodendron figo* or *Michelia frescata*).
Fula-freira ['fula 'frẹira] or ***fula-fresca*** ['fula 'frẹska] nun's orchid (*Phaius tankervilleae*).
Fula-laranjéra ['fula laraɲ'ǰẹra] orange blossom, used to decorate a bride's hair.
Fula-merénda ['fula

me'ręnda] flower of the crepe myrtle (*Lagerstroemia indica* or *Lagerstroemia alba*), formerly used in household remedies.

Fula-mogarim ['fula mǫgạ'riŋ] flower of the Arabian jasmine tree (*Jasminum sambac*).

Fula-mútri ['fula 'mutri] flower of the mock lemon tree (*Aglaia odorata* or *Aglaia mutre*).

Fula-papaia ['fula pa'pąia] papaya flower.

Fula-pavám ['fula pa'vaŋ] acacia flower.

Fula-pêdo ['fula 'pędu] flower in the skunk vine family (*Paederia foetida*). Also used for somebody who appears refined but is in fact vulgar.

Fula-sapatêro ['fula sapą'tęro] Chinese hibiscus (*Hibiscus rosa-sinensis*), also called <Chinese rose >. Its name derives from its use as shoepolish to stain leather black.

Fula-unha ['fula 'uɲa] ylang-ylang (*Artaborys odoratissimus*), climbing shrub giving rise to its name. 2. Vagina.

Fula-fula ['fula 'fula] *n*
Dessert made with rice, brown sugar and almonds.

Fumâ [fu'mạ] *vt*
To smoke.

Fumiga [fu'miga] *n*
Ant.

Fumigâ [fumi'gạ] *vi*
To feel pins and needles. *Fumigâ pê* to go to sleep (feet).

Fumo ['fumu] *n*
1. Smoke.
2. Black armband worn by men in mourning.

Fundéza [fun'dęza] *n*
Depth. *syn* **Fundura**.

Fundura [fun'dura] See **Fundéza**.

Furacám [fura'kaŋ] *n*
Hurricane.

Fura-vida ['fura 'vida] *n*
1. Adventurer.
2. Active person.

Fuzí [fu'zi] **fugí** [fu'ǰi] *vi*
To flee, escape.
❖***Já fuzí vêm*** [ǰa fu'zi vẹŋ] he fled here.
❖***Já fuzí vai*** [ǰa fu'zi vai] he escaped.

Fuzilâ [fuzi'lạ] *vi*
1. To dazzle.
2. To have an ambitious glint in the eye.

Fuzilada [fuzi'lạda] *n*
Flash produced by lightning.
Como fuzilada in a flash, like lightning.

Gabarolâ [gabarǫ'lạ] *vi*
To boast.
Gabarolâ onçóm [gabarǫ'lạ on'sọŋ] To boast of.

Gabirú [gąbi'ru] *adj & n*
1. Philanderer, libertine.
2. Fickle.

Gafinhâ [gąfi'ɲạ] *vt*
1. To search out, to ferret out, to find something difficult. *Úndi vôs já vai gafinhâ estung'a pintura?* where did you uncover this painting?
2. To tickle or scratch with fingernails.
Gafinhâ ôsso di bur-bur [gąfi'ɲạ 'ọso di bur'bur] used of an extremely nosy person who asks indiscrete questions. See **Bur-bur**.

Galado [ga'lądu] *adj*
Bewitched. See ***Ôlo galado***.

Galántaria [galanta'ria] *n*
Foppishness, affectation.

Galánte [gą'lanti] *adj*
1. Strange. Weird. *Sentí galánte* to feel out of place.
2. Extraordinary.
3. Extravagant.

Galinha [ga'liɲa] *adj & n*
1. Hen.
Galinha chacháu parida [ga'liɲa čą'čąw pa'rida] Macanese dish consisting of chicked cooked with ginger, wine and saffron. It is called *chacháu parida* in view of its supposed restorative properties for women after giving birth.
2. Low life woman. Prostitute.
❖ ***Galinha-choca*** [ga'liɲa 'čǫka] grumpy or raucous woman.

Galivante [gali'vạnti] *adj* (<*Eng. gallivant*)
1. Philanderer, libertine.
2. Fickle.

Galo-dôdo ['gąlu 'dọdu] *n*
1. Flirtatious, philandering.
2. Voluble, imprudent.

Gamafón [gama'fǫn] *n*
Gramophone.

Gambel [gąm'bęl] *n* (<*M. gambir*)
Leaf or resin from the gambiero, which used to be chewed along with **betel** and **areca**.

Gamên [ga'mẹn] See **Ganime**.

Ganchâ [gaɲ'čạ] *vt*
To hook.

Gandola [gạn'dǫla] *n*
Ridged luffa (*Luffa acutangula*), long green vegetable called <*si*[1] *kuá*[1] 絲瓜> in Chinese. It is eaten before it becomes ripe, since in its ripe form the flesh becomes fibrous and is used as a sponge for cleaning dishes. Hence it is also called *vegetable sponge* or *sponge gourd*.

Ganêro [gą'nẹro] *n* (<*C. kwan*[1] 關 + *P. -eiro*)
1. Formerly position as an intermediary in Macao's shipping trade.
2. Steward, sub-steward.

Ganim [ga'nim], **gamên** [ga'mẹn] *n* (<*C. ngan*[4] *nim*[6] 銀念)
Fruit of the *Dracontomelum sinense,* used in savoury preserves or **achar**, and in **sambal**, as a pickle.

Ganhâ [gą'ɲạ] *vi & vt*
To win. *Têm pa ganhâ* it's a winner, it's profitable. *Virâ mám, pode ganhâ* it can turn a profit in a flash of an eye.

Ganta ['gạnta] *n* (<*M. gantang*)
Malay measurement of weight, formerly used in Macao.

Gantaria [gạnta'ria] *n*
Person who focuses on insignificant details, nit picker.

Garganta [gạr'gạnta] *n*
Throat.

Garganta sêco [gąr'gạnta 'sẹku] to be thirsty.
Garganta largo [gąr'gạnta 'ląrgu] used to describe a person who takes advantage of another.

Gargú [gąr'gu] *n (<I.-P. gargó, <Kon. gādgó & <Mar. gādgá)*
1. Vessel for holding water.
2. Tumbler made of rough clay, for drinking tea.

Garida [gą'rida] *adj & n*
1. Coquette.
2. Presumptuous.
Garidóna [gąri'dọna] very coquettish.

Garidiça [gari'disa] *n*
1. Foppery.
2. Flirtation.

Gato ['gątu] *n*
Cat. *Gato fémea* female cat.
❖***Gato-manso*** ['gątu 'mạnsu] deceitful, traitorous.

Gato-som-som ['gątu sọŋ'sọŋ] *n*
Sweet preserve, formerly prepared in Macao convents.

Gatinhâ [gąti'ɲạ] *vi*
To crawl.

Gatunéro [gątu'nẹro] *n*
Cat-thief.

Gavartâ [gavąr'tạ] *vt*
To turn upside down, turn around.
Gavartâ armário to turn the wardrobe inside out.
Gavartâ ôsso di bur-bur [gavąr'tạ 'ọso di bur'bur] to go over or investigate with a magnifying glass.

Gazéta [gą'zẹta] *n*
1. Newspaper.
2. Bulletin.
❖***Gazetêro*** [gaze'tẹro] novelette.

Geléa [ǰe'lẹa] *n*
1. Calf's foot jelly.
2. Any kind of gelatine.

Gelêra [ǰe'lẹra] *n*
Refrigerator. See **Friza**.

Gemada [ǰe'mąda] *n*
Egg yolk, beaten with sugar.

Gente ['ǰęnti] *n*
People. *Gente-gente* people.
Gente falâ ['ǰęnti fą'lą] according to public opinion. *Têm gente falâ* some people say.
Gente grándi ['ǰęnti 'grandi] important people.
Gente bêm-fêto ['ǰęnti bęŋ 'fętu] refined people, people of good repute.

Genete ['ǰe'nęti] *n*
Cakes made around Christmas from cornflour, eggs and butter.

Geniado [ǰeni'adu] *adj*
Irate, angry.

Génio [ǰęniu] *n*
1. Character, nature, temperament. *Bôm génio* good-natured.
Génio di vilám ['ǰęniu di vi'laŋ] very bad-tempered.
2. Irritation, fury.
Subí génio [su'bi 'ǰęniu] to become irritated.
Levantâ génio [levan'tą 'ǰęniu] to get angry.

Goelâ [gwę'lą] *vi*
1. To shout.
2. To sing loudly.

Goelám [gwę'laŋ] *n*
Person who talks at the top of their voice.

Goita ['gǫita] *n*
Goitre.

Gomâ [gǫ'mą] *vt*
To stick, apply glue.

Gondôm [gǫn'dǫŋ] *n* (<*M. gondong*)
1. Spot or blister.
2. Boil.
3. Bump, swelling.
4. Fruit of the *arve di gondom*, weeping fig tree (*Ficus Benjamina*) common to Macao.

Gonchôm [gọŋ'gọŋ] *n* (<*M. goncang*)
To agitate, shake.

Gongôm[1] [gọŋ'gọŋ] *adj*
Stupid, idiotic.

Gongôm[2] [gọŋ'gọŋ] *n*
1. Twit, idiot. *Jêto di gongóm* stupid-looking.
2. May-bug.
3. Swelling, bump.

Gordofo [gor'dọfu] *n*
Corpulent man, cumbersome.

Gordofóna [gọrdo'fọna] *n*
Stout woman, voluminous.

Gorogotâ [gọrọgọ'tạ] *vi*
1. To be at death's door.
2. To die.

Gossô [gọ'sọ] *vi* (<*M. gosok*)
To mop, brush. *Gossô chám* to mop the floor.
To scrub, polish.

Gossodela [gọsọ'dẹla] *n* (<*M. gosok*)
1. Mop.
2. Wipe.

Gôsto ['gọstu] *n*
Flavour.
❖ ***Dâ gosto*** [dạ 'gọstu] to be fodder for gossip, to yield to pleasure.

Grám [graŋ] *n*
Grain. *Grám-grám* grains, grained.
❖ ***Arôz grám-grám*** [a'ros graŋ'graŋ] badly prepared rice.

Gramâ [grạ'mạ] *vt*
To put up with, tolerate. *Já gramâ qui tánto* he has put up with a lot. *Nôm pôde gramâ êle* I can't stand him.

Granzeâ [granzi'ạ] *vt*
To please in order to gain favour.

Grassâ [grạ'sạ] *vt*
To polish. *Grassâ bota* to polish boots.

Greta [‘gręta] *n*
Split, fissure.

Gréza [‘gręza] *n*
Church. *Corê greza* to go to several churches on Maundy Thursday.

Gritâ [gri’tạ] *vi*
1. To shout. *Já gritâ co iou* he shouted with me.
2. To call. *Gritâ pa vôs* to call out for you.

Grog [grǫg] *n* (<*Eng. grog*)
Alcoholic drink.

Grogomilo [grogo’milu] *n*
Gullet, throat.

Guardâ [guạr’dạ] *vt*
To put away, hide.
❖***Guardâ gaja*** [guạr’dạ ‘gạǰa] (i) to have an affair; (ii) to have an extramarital affair.

Gudám [gu’daŋ] *n* (<*M. gudang*)
1. Ground floor.
2. Basement.
3. Store.
4. Shop.

Guínde [‘gindi] *n*
Jug. *Guínde di águ* jug of water.

Gunde [‘gundi] See **Gúni**.

Gúni [‘guni], **gunde** [‘gundi] *n* (<*Mar./C. gon*)
Thick sack for storing rice or sand. Also called **saco gúni** or **saco gúndi**.

Guní [gu’ni] *vi*
To growl.

Gurunhâ [guru’ɲạ] *vi*
To gumble, to mumble, to complain in a low voice. *Procópio nôm têm fim di gurunhâ vai, gurunhâ vêm* Procópio never stops moaning.

Hambâc [hạm'bạk] See **ambâc**.

Ham-chi-su [hạm či'su] *n* (<*C. ham⁴ chi¹ sou¹* 鹹雞酥)
Sweet and savoury Chinese cake similar to biscuit.

Hám-chói [hạm'čọi] *n* (<*C. ham⁴ choi³* 鹹菜)
Pickled vegetables.

Hám-sâp-lou [hạm sạp'lọ] *adj* (<*C. ham⁴ sab¹ lou²* 鹹濕佬)
Lascivious, depraved, libidinous.

Helâ [ẹ'la] See **Elâ** [ẹ'la]

Hirói [i'rọi] *n*
Hero.

Home ['ọmi] *n*
Man. *Home-home di hoze* men nowadays.

Homezarám [ọmiza'raŋ] *n*
Big built man.

Hong-tau-chôc [họŋ tạu'čọk] *n* (<*C. hong⁴ tau⁶ chok⁷* 紅豆粥)
Sweet soup prepared with beans and raw sugar.

Hónra ['ọŋra] *n*
Honour.

Horta ['ọrta] *n*
Orchard.

Hortelám [ọrte'laŋ] *n*
Mint. *Hortelám di sopa* spearmint (*Mentha viridis*). *Hortelám malavar* lavender (*Anisochilus carnosus*).

Hotê [o'tẹ] *n*
Hotel.

Hoze ['ọzi], ['ọji] *adv*
Today. *Hoze sâm domingo* it's Sunday today.

Hui [wi] *n* (<*C. wui²* 會)
1. Quota system.
2. Association.
3. System of loans in which twelve or more members are involved. They contribute a

fixed amount of money on a regular basis to create a "cake" which can then be used by the member who offers the highest rate of interest to the others.

Cabeça di hui [ka'bęsa di wi] chairperson of a **hui**.

Filo-di-hui ['filu di wi] member of a **hui**.

Humiliâ [umili'ạ] *vt*

1. To humiliate.
2. To vex.
3. To embarass.

Humiliaçám [umilia'saŋ] *n*

Humiliation.

Ia [ya] *adv*
Ia emphasizes an imminent action. *Tâ vâi-ia,* I'll be right there!

Iam-chá [yąm'čą] *n* (<*C. yam*[2] *cha*[4] 飲茶)
Chinese meal served between breakfast and lunchtime.

Iam-chi-cu [yąm či'ku] *n* (<*C. hum*[4] *tsi*[4] *ku*[1] 咸茨菇)
Chinese vegetable.

Iau chá kuai [yąw čą'kwąi] *n* (<*C. yau*[4] *tsa*[3] *gwai*[2] 油炸鬼)
Chinese fritter.

Ico ['iku] *n*
Diminutive of Teodorico or Frederico.

Ilarga [i'lągrga] *prep*
Beside.

Ilôtro [i'lọtru] *pron*
They.
Ilôtro-sua or *ilôtro-sa* his, her, their.

Image [i'mąǰi] *n*
1. Image.
2. Statue.

Imbigo [im'bigu] See **Umbigo**.

Impachâ [impą'čą] *vt*
To fill. *Impachâ estômo* to eat one's fill.

Impada [im'pąda], **empada** [ẹm'pąda] *n*
Pie filled with fish or chicken and olives, at Christmas.

Impê [im'pẹ] See **Empê**.

Impestâ [impẹs'tą] *vi*
To exhale stale breath. See also **Fêde**.

Impido [im'pidu] See **Empido**.

Impinâ [impi'ną] *vt*
1. To lift up.
2. To stretch.

Impinhâ [impi'ɲą] *vt*
To pawn.

Impostôr [impǫs'tǫ] *adj*
Vain, proud.

Imposturice [impǫstu'risi] *n*
1. Vanity.
2. Ostentation.

Imprensâ [impreŋ'sạ] *vt*
1. To print.
2. To publish.

Incachâ [iŋką'čạ] *vt*
1. To fit in.
2. To insert.

Incacho [iŋ'kąču] *n*
Diaper.

Inchí [iɲ'či], **enchê** ['ẹɲ'čẹ] *vt*
To fill. *Já inchí vinho na buiám* he filled up the wine flask.

Inchido [iɲ'čidu] *adj*
1. Full.
2. Replete

Ingulí [iŋgu'li] *vt*
To swallow, gulp. *Ingulí comê* he gulps his food down.

Inhame [i'ɲami] See **nhame**.

Inovaçám [inova'saŋ] *n*
Innovation.

Insaguâ [insą'gwạ], **inxaguâ** [iɲšą'guạ] *vt*
To rinse.
❖ ***Insaguâ vista*** [iɲsą'gwạ 'vista] (i) to enjoy looking at some pleasing thing or person; (ii) to have a wandering eye.

Intacâ [intą'kạ] *vt*
To force feed, stuffing the mouth with liquid or solids.

Intalâ [intą'lạ] *vt*
1. To entrap.
2. To compromise, ensnare. *Intalâ na iou* he caught me out.

Intremente [intre'mẹnti] *adv & conj*
While. *Intremente ilôtro tâ comê* while they are eating.

Intresmentes [intre'mẹntes] *adv & conj*
In the meantime.

Intrudo [in'trudu] *n*
Carnival.

Intulâ [intu'lạ] *vt*
1. To pile up.
2. To stuff with food.

Inventaçám [iŋventa'saŋ] *n*
1. Invention.
2. Invented story or novelty.
3. Lie.

Iou [yọw] See **Io**.

Io [yọ], **iou** [yọw] *pron*
1. I.
2. Me. *Dâ iou* give me. *Maria já olâ co iou* Maria saw me. *Sâm sô pa iou* this is just for me. *Vêm co iou* come with me. ***Iou-sua*** ['yọw sua] or ***iou-sa*** ['yọw sa] mine. *Iou-sua pai* my father. *Iou-sua fila* my daughter. See **Sa**.

Irmandade [irman'dạdi] *n*
1. Brothers, siblings. *Irmandade quelê unido* close siblings.
2. Religious brotherhood.

Iscapâ [iskạ'pạ] *vi*
To escape. *Iscapâ morrê* to escape death by the skin of one's teeth.

Iscutâ [isku'tạ] *vt*
To peep, see. *Já iscutâ na buraco di porta* he snooped through the keyhole. *Vêm iscutâ pa iou* come and see me.

Iscuta [is'kuta] *n*
1. Sly look, glance.
2. Visit. *Dâ ung'a iscuta* to visit.

Ismerâ [izmẹ'rạ] *vi*
To do one's best.

Ismifrâ [izmi'frạ] *vt*
1. To use somebody else's money.
2. To spend down to the last cent.

Ismirado [izmi'rạdu] *adj*
Wizened, dried up. *Seco ismirado* completely withered.

Ispalâ [ispą'lą] *vt*

1. To spread.
2. To divulge.

Ispêlo [is'pęlu] *n*

Mirror. *Nôm têm ispêlo na casa?* don't you have a mirror at home? *Pegâ ispêlo* to pick up a mirror, look in the mirror. ❖***Mesa-ispêlo*** ['męza is'pęlo] dressing table.

Isquevê [iskę'vę] *vt*

To write. *Isquevê dós regra pa iou* drop me a couple of lines.

Istrica [is'trika] See **Estrika**.

Istricâ [istri'ką] See **Estrikâ**.

Isvazâ [izvą'zą] *vt*

To empty.

Izalâ [izą'lą] *vt*

To exhale.

Izizí [izi'zi] *vt*

To demand.

Já [ǰa] *adv*

1. Already. Used with a verb, **já** indicates that the action, usually in the past, has been completed. Placing **já** before a verb in the past tense is optional. *Iou já falâ* I spoke. *Vôs já uví?* have you heard? *Tudo já vai* they all went. *Atútu já vêm di América* Artur has come back from America, *Chico-Chai já casâ* Chico-Chai got married, *iou já falâ* I spoke.

❖ ***Já têm-ia!*** [ǰa 'tẹŋ ya] it's fine, I've got it! Expression used when a solution to a problem or an idea has been found.

❖ ***Já olâ*** [ǰa o'lạ] do you see? do you understand?

2. Repeated at the beginning of consecutive phrases, **já** means <now (this way) ... now (that)>. *Já churâ, já rí* both laughing and crying.

Jaca ['ǰaka] *n* (<*Mal. chakka*)

Jack fruit (*Artocarpus integrifolia*).

Jagra ['ǰạgra] *n*

Muscovado sugar, from either the palm or sugarcane, sold in caramel-coloured tablets. An important component in various Macanese desserts.

❖ ***Vai comê jagra!*** [vai kọ'mẹ 'ǰagrạ] go to hell!, get lost!

Jambo ['ǰambu] *n* (<*M. & Sanskr. jambu*)

Rose-apple (*Syzgyzium jambos Alston Myrtaceae*). Yellowish tropical fruit, the size of a tangerine.

Jambúa [ǰạm'bua] *n* (<*M. jambua*)

Grapefuit (*Citrus decumana*).

Jambulám [ǰambu'laŋ] *n* (<*M. jamblang*)

Jamun fruit (*Eugenia jambolana*) from India, the size of a black grape or olive and now rarely found in Macao. It is believed to have medicinal properties, and that its seeds can treat diabetes.

Janéro [ǰa'nęro] *n*
January.

Jangôm [ǰaŋ'gǫŋ] *n* (<*M. janggong*)
1. Corn.
2. Cob.

Janota [ǰa'nǫta] adj
Elegant, chic.

Janotâ [ǰanǫ'tạ] *vi*
To dress well, to be well turned-out.

Janotismo [ǰano'tizmo] *n*
Elegance, great aplomb.

Jaqueta [ǰa'kęta] *n*
Man's jacket.

Jenjum [ǰeɲ'j‡uŋ] *n*
Fasting.

Jêto ['ǰẹtu] *adv*
Way, manner.
Jêto qui ['ǰẹtu ki] it looks like. *Jêto qui tâ querê* it looks like she wants it.

Joaquim-Sucre [ǰoa'kiŋ 'sukri] *adj*
Lady-killer.

Jota ['ǰǫta] *n*
1. Japanese.
2. Macao's Judiciary Police Force agent.

Jóvi ['ǰǫvi] *adj*
Young

Juda ['ǰuda] *n*
Judas.

Judâ [ǰu'dạ] *vi*
To help. *Judâ iou cartâ estung'a quanto mala-mala* help me carry these suitcases.

Jugâ [ǰu'gạ] *vt*
1. To play.
❖***Jogâ sôco*** [ǰu'gạ 'soku] to hit or punch.
2. To gamble.

Jugadéra [ǰuga'dęra] *n*
Female gambler. Woman who likes to gamble.

Júlio ['ǰuliu] *n*

July.

Júnio ['ǰuniu] *n*

June.

Juntâ [ǰun'tạ] *vt*

To gather. *Juntâ rancho* (i) to form a group; (ii) to keep bad company. *Juntâ sapeca* to save money, be economical.

Juntado [ǰun'tą̣du] *adj*

1. Joined, together.
2. Saved (in money).

Juro! ['ǰuro] *adv*

Honestly! God's truth!

Justeza [ǰus'tęza] *n*

Justness, justice.

Justo ['ǰustu] *adj & adv*

1. Right, correct.
2. Precisely, rightly.

Justo pa justo ['ǰustu pa 'ǰustu] thoroughly.

Labitâ [labi'tạ], **lapitâ** [lapi'tạ] *vt*
1. To speak.
Capaz labitâ he can speak well.
2. To parrot.

Lacassá [ląka'są] *n* (<*M. laksa*)
Vermicelli.

Ladéra [la'dęra] *n*
Slope, incline. *Qui pussâ bafado subí acung'a ladéra!* I'm quite out of breath going up that slope!

Ladinha [la'diɲa] *n*
1. Litany.
2. Lengthy scolding, tiresome conversation.
Uví mai-sua ladinha to listen to a mother's scolding.

Ladino [la'dinu] *adj*
1. Astute.
2. Smart. *Quiança ladino* quick-witted child.

Ladrám-pinto [lą'draŋ 'pintu] *n*
Bird of prey, kind of hawk.

Ladú [lą'du] *n* (<*Kon. ládū*)
Macanese dessert made at Carnival with glutinous rice, raw sugar, roast pinenuts and coconut.
❖ ***Cara di ladú*** ['kara di lą'du] used to describe a woman who uses too much make-up, recalling the appearance of the dessert.

Lagartiâ ['lagąrti'ạ] *vi*
To stretch; to lie down.

Lágri ['lągri] *n*
Tears. *Lágri cacho-cacho* to weep buckets of tears. *Lágri di crocodilo* crocodile tears, hypocrite.

Lagrimado [lagri'mądu] *adj*
Tearful, crying.

Laia ['lạya], **leia** ['lẹya] *n*
1. Kind, category, type. *Laia-laia* assorted, selection. *Tudo laia* all kinds, all qualities.
2. Manner, mode. *Destung'a laia* this way.

Lailai-faifai [lai'lai fai'fai] *adv*
Hurried or disorderly way of doing things.

Laissí [lai'si] *n* (<*C. lei*^{6} *si*^{6} *利事*)
Money, (usually a small amount), placed in a red envelope decorated with auspicious characters. Given by Chinese to relatives and friends at celebrations, especially Lunar New Year, to wish them happiness and good health.

Lám[1] [ląm] *n* (<*C. lam*^{2} *欖*)
Chinese fruit, similar to an olive and eaten either sweet or savoury.

Lám[2] [laŋ] *n*
Wool. *Tecê lám* to weave. *Bola di lám* ball of wool.

Lambicha [lam'biča] *adj*
Dishonest person.

Lambiscâ [lambis'ką] *vt*
To chip, crack. *Estung'a vun qui lambiscado* this bowl is all chipped around the rim.

Lameado [lami'ądu] *adj*
1. Dirty.
2. Muddied, muddy.

Lampiám [lampi'aŋ] *n*
Lamp, traditionally lit with kerosene or peanut oil.

Lampita [lam'pita] *adj*
Nosy, busy-body. See **Chuchumeca**.

Lanchâi [laɲ'čąi] *n* (<*C. lan*^{6} *chai*^{2} *爛仔*)
1. Street kid.
2. Ruffian; hooligan.

Lape ['ląpi] *n* (<*M. lapis*)
Layer, covering.

Lápi-lápi ['ląpi 'ląpi] *adj*
1. Disintegrating.
2. Hanging.

Lapitâ [lapi'tą] See **Labitâ**.

Laranja pagode [la'rąɲǰa pą'gǫdi] *n*
Kumquat (*Fortunella margarita*).

Largâ [ląr'gạ] *vt*
1. To leave, abandon, go away. *Largâ calçám* for boys of a certain age who moved into wearing long trousers rather than shorts.
❖***Largâ verde, caçâ maduro*** [ląr'gạ 'verdi | ka'sạ ma'duru] to gain information from a slight hint.
2. To give birth.

Latagám [ląta'gaŋ] *n*
A big man.

Lau-chai [law'čại] *n* (<*C. lau*[3] *tsa*[2] 樓宅)
Mezzanine floor in a small house.

Lavadéra [ląva'dęra] *n*
Washerwoman who would collect laundry from private houses.

Leám [li'aŋ] *n*
Lion. *Leám na cajola* a caged lion.

Leca ['lęka] *n*
Pataca, the value of a pataca. - *Quanto custâ? - Barato, três léca ná-más!* – How much is it? – It's cheap, only three patacas! See **Rúfa**.

Lecenço [le'sęnsu] *n*
Boil, pimple.

Leia ['lęya] See **Laia**.

Lencó [lęŋ'kǫ], **leng-kok** [lęŋ'kǫk˥] *n* (<*C. leng*[4] *kok*[3] 棱角)
Variety of water chestnut (*Trapa bicornis*).

Leng-kok [lęŋ'kǫk˥] See **Lencó**.

Leong-fan [lioŋ'fạn] *n* (<*C. leong*[4] *fan*[2] 涼粉)
Chinese herb jelly made from black agar-agar.

Leongfanêro [lioŋ'fạnẹro] *n* (<*C. leong*[4] *fan*[2] 涼粉 + *P. -ero*)
Chinese diver who collects oysters from the muddy waters of Macao and cracks them open.

Lésa[1] ['lęza] *adj*
Excessively sensitive.

Lésa[2] ['lęza] *n*
Softy.

Letrado [le'tradu] *n*
1. Lawyer.
2. Educated man.
3. Poet.

Levantâ [levạn'tạ] *vt*
To clear. *Levantâ mesa* to clear the table.

Levantâ [levạn'tạ] *vt*
1. To get up, rise.
2. To raise.
❖ ***Levantâ ira*** [levạn'tạ 'ira] to become infuriated. *Nê-bôm bulí co iou-sa pai, êle tâ levantâ ira* don't cross my father because he is very irritated.
❖ ***Levantâ fedôr*** [levạn'tạ fẹ'dọ] *syn* **Levantâ ira**.

Lichia [li'čia] *n* (<*C. lai*[6] *tsi*[1] 荔枝)
Lychee (*Litchi chinensis*).

Lichim [li'čiŋ] *adj* (<*M. licin*)
1. Slippery.
2. Smooth. *Pêle liching* smooth skin.

Limpado [lim'padu] *adj*
Clean.
Pobre cú limpado ['pọbri ku lim'padu] (i) poor soul. (ii) empty pockets.

Lin-ngau [lin 'ŋạu] *n* (<*C. Lin*[4] *ngau*[2] 蓮藕)
Lotus root.

Língu ['liŋgu] *n*
1. Tongue.
Língu caregado ['liŋgu kare'gadu] affected way of

speaking Portuguese, rolling the ‘r’s.

Língu marado [‘liŋgu ma’radu] babytalk.

Língu di prata [‘liŋgu di ‘pr̨ata] silver-tongued.

Língu torto [‘liŋgu ’tọrtọ] speech defect.

2. Language.

Língua nhom [‘liŋgwa ɲọɲ] See **Patuá**.

Língua nhônha [‘liŋgwa ‘ɲọɲa] See **Patuá**.

Linguaréra [liŋgwa’r̨era] *n*
Gossip.

Liu-liu [liu’liu] *n & vt* (<*C. liu² liu²* 撩撩)
1. Chinese oar.
2. Chinese rowing boat.
3. To row.

Liu-pun [liu’pun] *n* (<*C. liu⁶ pun³* 料半)
Chinese rice wine.

Lôgo¹ [‘lọgo] *adv*
Later.

Lôgo² [‘lọgo] *adv*
Necessarily. Used with a verb, **lôgo** indicates an action in the future.
Iou lôgo vai I will go. *Vôs lôgo olâ* you will see. *Quim lôgo dâ?* who will give?

Lôgomente [lọgo’menti] *adv*
1. Immediately.
2. Quickly. *Justo chegâ casa, lôgomente sai* as soon as he returned home, he went out again.

Lombo [‘lombo] *n*
1. Rib.
2. Chop. *Lombo pó di bolacho* pork cutlet.

Long-ngán [loŋ ’ŋąn] *n* (<*C. long⁴ ngán²* 龍眼)
Longan fruit (*Nephelium longana*).

Lo-pac-cou [lọ pą’kou] *n* (<*C. lo⁴ pak⁹ kou¹* 蘿蔔糕)

Turnip cake. See also **Bebinca**, ***bebinca-rábano***.

Lorcha [‘lǫrča] *n*

Small Chinese rowing boat. *Lorcha grande* (i) junk; (ii) sailing boat. *Lorcha-potóm* shaped like a **lorcha**. See **Potóm**.

Lugâ [lu’gạ] *vi*

To rent. *Êle já lugâ ung’a casa na vánda di Lilau* he rented a house in Lilau.

Lúmi [‘lumi] *adj*

1. Lit.
2. Illuminated.

Lustro [‘lustro] *adj*

1. Shiny.
2. Bright.

❖ ***Ólo lustro*** [ǫlo ‘lustro] clear-eyed, lustful gaze, mischeivous eyes.

Maçám nanquim [ma'saŋ naŋ'kiŋ] *n*
Jujube (*Ziziphus Jujuba*), called <*mat*[9] *chou*[2] 蜜棗> in Cantonese.

Maca ['mąka] *n*
1. Stretcher.
2. Ambulance.

Macaco [ma'kąku] *n*
Monkey.
❖ ***Macaco imitaçám*** [ma'kąku imita'saŋ] mimic.
❖ ***Macaco vêlo*** [ma'kąku 'vẹlu] smarty-pants.
❖ ***Macaco sêco*** [ma'kąku 'sẹku] extremely thin. There is a semantic parallel in the Cantonese <*ma*[5] *lau*[1] *kon*[1] 馬騮竿>.

Macaio [ma'kąyu] *n*
Same as *macaense* (Macanese), somebody born in Macao. Pejorative expression used by metropolitan Portuguese to describe the Luso-Chinese descendants born in Macao. The term was also used amongst the Macanese to mean a Macanese of low status.

Macaísta [maka'ista] See **Maquista**.

Macau-filo [mą'kąw 'filu] *n*
Macanese, born in Macao, son of the earth.

Macau-paio [mą'kąw 'pąyu] *n*
Pejorative name given to Macanese by the **tom-tom,** Macanese based in Hong Kong.

Macazote [mąka'zǫti], **marcazote** [mąrka'zǫti] *n*
Sponge cake.

Macho fémea ['mąču·'fẹmia] *n*
1. Ponce.
2. Butch woman.
3. Tomboy.

Macupa [ma'kupa] *n*
Kind of rose-apple, called <*pôu*[4] *tôu*[4] 葡萄> in Chinese.

Maçombrado [mąsǫm'brądu] *adj*
Haunted. *Más bôm nádi vivo na acung'a casa, assí maçombrado!* it's better not to live in this haunted house.

Mafomaria [mąfǫma'ria] *n*
Sorcery, witchcraft.

Mai [mại] *n*
Mother. *Tudo mai-mai* all mothers.
Mai di casa ['mại di 'kąza] housekeeper, servant in charge of all domestic affairs.

Mainato [mai'nątu] *n* (<*Mal. mannattan*)
1. Chinese laundryman who takes washing in.
2. Laundry.

Mala tampípi ['mąla tam'pipi] *n* (<*P. mala* + *M. tampi/tampin*)
Rattan or cane suitcase which was formerly commonly used by Macanese families.

Malau [mą'lạw] *n* (<*C. ma² lau¹ 馬騮*)
Monkey.
Malau cón [mą'lạw kǫn] (i) skinny man; (ii) *fig* slender person.

Ma-língu [mą 'liŋgu] *n*
Gossiper. *Vôs sã bem di má língu* what a gossiper you are.

Malínguâ [mąliŋ'gwą] *vt*
To speak ill of others. *Tudo dia malinguâ* he/she spends all day tittle-tattling. *Chiquita boca-rôto qui nôm pôde más, nôm têm fim di malinguâ pa tudo vánda!* Chiquita can't keep a secret, she spends her days gossipping right, left and centre.

Mal-pôsto [mąl·'pǫstu] *adj*
1. Shabby.
2. Poorly turned-out.
See also **Bêm**, ***Bêm-pôsto***.

Mám [maŋ] *n*
1. Hand. *Pê-mám* hand and foot.
❖***Mám-fichado*** [maŋ fi'čądu] miserly, tight-fisted.

Mám fichado qui fichado [maŋ fi'čądu ki fi'čądu] mean, miserly. *Êle mám fichado qui fichado, nádi gastâ sapeca* he is very thrifty, he won't part with a penny.
❖***Mám tánto*** [maŋ·'tąntu] meddler.
Mám cumprido [maŋ kum'pridu] (i) thief; (ii) sticky-fingered, prone to stealing.
Mám di fada [maŋ di 'fada] nimble-fingered.
❖***Mám pa trás*** [maŋ pa 'trąs] (i) idle-handed; (ii) *fig* leisurely, lazy person.
Pegâ mám andâ rua [pę'gą maŋ an'dą 'rua] to stroll hand in hand.
❖***Cai pê-mám*** [kąi pę'maŋ] (i) to lose one's temper; (ii) to become lost.
❖ ***Mám-lárgo*** [maŋ 'ląrgu] generous.
❖***Mám-macaco*** [maŋ ma'kąku] fidgety.
❖ ***Mám-fêde*** [maŋ 'fęde] somebody with a dirty mind.
2. Arm.

Mám-cutí [maŋ ku'ti] *n* (<*P. mão* + *M. kuti*)
Doorknob.

Mám-di-buda [maŋ di 'buda] *n*
Bergamot (*Citrus bergamia*), called <*fat^{9} sáu^{2} kâm^{1} 佛手柑*> in Chinese.

Mamâ[1] [ma'mą] *n*
Mummy, mother.

Mamâ[2] [ma'mą] *vt*
To suckle.

Mamám [mą'maŋ] *n*
Parishioner of St. Anthony's parish in Macao. Also referred to as **Mamám di Sant'António**.

Mamá-sógra [mą'ma 'sǫgra] *n*
Mother-in-law. *Mamá-sogra sã mai di vôs-sa siara* your mother-in-law is your wife's mother.

Mámi ['mąmi] *n* (<*Eng. mummy*)
Mummy, mother.

Mamún [mą'mun] *n*
Cakes made with rice flour and beaten eggs.

Mana ['mąna] *n*
Older sister.

Mandante [man'dąnti] *n*
1. Commander.
2. Leader, instigator.

Manduco [mąn'duko] *n* (<*Kon. māndūk*)
Toad, frog.

Manejante [mąne'ǰąnti] *n* (<*Eng. manager*)
Manager, director. *Más bôm trabalâ-ia manejante têm aqui!* we better get to work, the boss is here!

Mangustám [mąŋgus'taŋ] *n*
Mangosteen (*Garcinia mangostana*), originally from Malaysia.

Mangericám [maŋǰerikaŋ] *n*
Basil (*Ocimum gratissimum*).

Máno ['mąnu] *n*
1. Older brother.
2. Older son.

Manquenfum [mąŋkeŋ'fuŋ], **maquinfum** [makiŋ'fuŋ] *n* (<*C. man⁶ keng¹ fong¹* 慢惊風)
Ill air that can cause certain diseases.

Maquinfum [makiŋ'fuŋ] See **Manquenfum**.

Mánta ['mąnta] *n*
Shawl.

Mapeça [mą'pęsa] *n*
1. Tasteless joke.
2. Joke. *Fazê mapeça* to play a joke.

Mapeçoso [mape'soso] *adj & n*
Intentionally irritating or contrary.

Maquiâ [mąki'ą] *vt*
To spoil a child.

Maquiaçám [mąkia'saŋ] *n*
Impoliteness. *Fazê maquiaçám* to be rude.

Maquinéta [maki'nęta] *n*
Gasoline, used for heating water or for cooking.

Maquista [mą'kista], **macaísta** [maka'ista] *n*
1. Macanese, born in Macao.
2. Macanese, Luso-Chinese descendant.
3. **Patuá**, Macao Creole. *Língu maquista* Macanese Creole, to talk about the Macanese.
Maquista chapado [mą'kista ča'pądu] pure Macanese.

Marâ [mą'rạ] *vt*
To anchor, to link.
Marâ chiquía [mą'rạ či'kia] to tie one's hair up.
Marâ corda [mą'rạ 'kǫrda] to tie with string.
❖ ***Marâ casamênto*** [mą'rạ kaza'męntu] (i) to arrange a marriage; (ii) to become engaged.
❖ ***Marâ par*** [mą'rạ pąr] to put on a par.

Marado[1] [ma'rądu] *adj*
Tied up.
Cintura marado [sin'tura ma'rądu] corseted.
Pê marado [pę ma'rądu] bound feet.

Marado[2] [ma'rądu] *n*
Package.
Cartâ marado [kąr'tạ ma'rądu] to carry packages.

Marcazote [mąrka'zǫti] See **macazote**.

Mardigota [mardi'gǫta] *n*
Epilepsy.

Margo ['mąrgọ] *adj*
Bitter.

Margura [mar'gura] *n*
Bitterness.

Mariscâ [mąris'kạ] *vi*
To snack.

Maroto [ma'rotu] See **Belis maroto**.

Más [mąs] *adv*
More.

Más-a-más more and more. *Si más pricisâ* if more is needed. ***Más bôm*** [mąs 'bọŋ] better. ***Más grándi*** [mąs 'grandi] bigger.

Masquí [mas'ki] *adv*
1. In spite of.
2. Although. *Masquí seza* although it is like that.
3. Let it be.

Mata-moça ['mąta 'mọsa] *n*
Spinach.

Matâ-morê [mą'tą mọ'rẹ] *vi*
1. To make a huge effort, work oneself down to the bone.
2. To try, succeed.

Mate ['mąti] *n (<M. mati, <Kon. māti)*
Clay, mud.

Mau [mąw] *adv*
Bad.
Mau coraçám [mąw kọra'saŋ] person who wishes somebody ill. *Êle qui mau coraçám* he is so bad.
Mau repente [mąw re'pẹnti] (i) impulsive; (ii) rash action inspired by a bad temper.

Mâz [mąz] *conj*
1. But, however.
2. Nevertheless.

Me [me] *adv*
Expletive particle expressing supplication. *Comê-me!* Go on, eat!

Mea ['mea] *n*
Stocking, sock.

Mechâ [me'šą] *vt*
To gratify.

Medónha [mẹ'dọɲa] *adj*
Awful, terrible.

Meo ['meu] *n*
1. Middle. *Na meo di rua* in the middle of the street.
2. Half. *Meo porçolana* a half-bowl. *Pataca meo* one and a half patacas.

Mercê [mẹr'sẹ]
Thanks to.

Têm mercê [tẹŋ mẹr'sẹ] (i) he is entitled; (ii) it is worthy.

Messâ [mẹ'sạ] *vt*
To threaten.

Mestê [mes'tẹ] *v*
It's necessary, it has to be. ***Nomestê*** or ***nôm mestê*** [nomẹs'tẹ] (i) should not; (ii) it's not necessary. *Nomestê réva* you shouldn't get angry.

Mestre ['mestri] *n*
Master, teacher.
Mestre-china ['mestri 'čina] Chinese healer.

Metê [mẹ'tẹ] *vt*
1. To put.
2. To place.
❖***Metê fogo*** [mẹ'tẹ 'fọgo] (i) to instigate; (ii) to incite disorder.

Miao-miao [myạw 'myạw] *n*
Meow, mewing.
❖***Miao-miao sâm nosso gato!*** [myạw 'myạw sạŋ 'nọso 'gạtu] he might talk, he might moan, but he's still ours!

Miçó ['misọ] See **Missó**.

Militário [mili'tạriu] *n* (<*Eng. military*)
Infantry soldier (term from Hong Kong).

Minap [mi'nap] *n* (<*C. min^4 nap^6 棉衲*)
Chinese padded jacket.

Mínchi ['miɲči] *n*
Traditional Macanese dish made with minced pork or beef and fried with onion and other condiments.

Min-pau [min'pạw] *n* (<*C. min^6 麵 + P. pão 包*)
Bread. *Min-pau quente-quente* warm bread, fresh out of the oven.
See also **Pâm**.

Mintói [min'tọi] *adj & n* (<*C. min^4 toi^1 棉胎*)
Miserly.

Misco ['misku] *adj & n*
Miserly, mean.

Misquinhâ [miski'ɲạ] *vt*
1. To be a spendthrift.
2. To save.

Misquinho [mis'kiɲu] *adj*
1. Miserly.
2. Thrifty.

Missa-galo ['misa 'gạlu] *n*
Midnight mass, the first Christmas mass, at midnight on the 24th of December.

Missó, miçó ['misọ] *n* (<*J. miso*)
Paste made of soybeans and salt. See also **chili missó**. *Missó cristám* Macanese dish made with a base of soybeans, minced pork and saffron.

Mizâ [mi'zạ] *vi*
To urinate.
❖ ***Mizâ-coâ*** [mi'zạ co'ạ] money-grubbing.

Mizinha [mi'ziɲa] *n*
Home-made remedy or medication. *Mizinha saván* homemade remedy for **saván**. *Mizinha vento* medication to cure ailments brought on by ill airs.

Mizo ['mizu] *n*
Urine.
❖***Mizo di padre cura*** ['mizu di 'pạdri 'kura] Very weak tea.

Mocorô [moko'rọ] *n*
Soapnut (*Sapindus mukorossi*), formerly used to wash clothes.

Moça ['mọsạ] *n f*, **moço** ['mọso] *n m*
1. African servant or slave kept formerly in wealthy houses.
2. Very young Chinese servant.

Moço ['mọso] See **Moça**.

Môfo ['mọfo] *n*
1. Mould.
2. Musty smell.

Mogarim [mọga'riŋ], **mungarim** [muŋga'riŋ] *n* (<*Kon./Mar. mogrém*)

Arabian jasmine (*Jasminum sambac*).

Mol-mol [mọl'mọl] *n*
Fine white cambric used in olden times to make women's underclothing.

Mongus [mọŋ'gus] *adj* (<*M. mungkus*)
1. Sad.
2. Looking down.

Môno ['mọno] *adj*
Idiot, twit.

Mordecim [morde'siŋ] *n*
1. Headache caused by unknown source.
2. Ailment causing strong headaches.
3. Indisposition. *Atacâ mordecim* to suffer an indisposition.
❖ ***Raspâ mordecim*** [rąs'pą mordi'siŋ] old folk remedy for treating **mordecim**, in which the skin is scraped with a copper coin to as to bring the blood up to the surface and make a bruise. Called <*kuat*[8] *sa*[1] 刮痧> in Chinese.

Morê [mọ'rẹ] *vi*
To die.

Morna ['mọrna] *adj*
Lukewarm, tepid. *Águ morna* tepid water.

Môro ['mọrọ] *n*
1. Mahratta.
Môro-chut ['mọrọ čut] Sikh.
2. Muslim.
3. Any person from India who is not a Christian.

Mortificâ [mortifi'kạ] *vi*
To sacrifice oneself.

Muchâ [mu'čạ] *vi*
To wither.

Múchi ['muči] *n*
Rice cake made from **arôz pulú** and filled with dessicated coconut, roasted beans and sesame. See **Apa**, ***apa múchi***.

Mucho [‘mučo], **murcho** [‘murčo] *adj*
Withered. *Mucho qui mucho* already withered.
Mucho como hám-chói [‘mučo ‘komo hąm’čhọi] dejected, defeated. See **Hám-chói**.

Mufinâ [mufi’nạ] *vi*
To curse, bring bad luck, bode ill. *Qui-foi mufinâ?* Why are you swearing? Why are you casting bad luck around?

Mufinaze [mufi’nązi] *n*
Bad luck, ill omen.

Mufino[1] [mu’finu] *adj*
Troublesome, discomfitting.

Mufino[2] [mu’finu] *n*
Miserable person, person who is a bad omen. *Vai-nâ, mufino!* Go away, you waster!

Mui [mwi] *n (<C. mui^4 梅)*
Plum.
Mui cafre [mwi ‘kafri] black plum, called <*hak^7 mui^4 黑梅*> in Chinese.
Mui garganta [mwi gar‘ganta] kind of **mui**, also called ***mui azêdo*** and used for treating sore throats. Called <*sun^1 mui^4 酸梅*> in Chinese.
Vistido como dóci di mui [vis’tido ‘kọmo ‘dọsi di·mwi] very natty.

Mulâ [mu’lạ] *vt*
To soak.
Sopa-sopa mulado [‘sọpa·’sọpa mu’lądu] soaked through, completely drenched.
❖ ***Mulâ goela*** [mu’lạ ‘gwęla] to have a drink.

Mulé [mu’lę] *n*
Woman. *Mulé-mulé* women.
Marido mulé [mą’ridu mu’lę] (i) man and wife; (ii) couple.

Mungo [‘muŋgọ] *n (<Kon./Mar. muūg, Hindust. muūng)*
Mung bean (*Phaseolus aureus*).

Murcho [‘murčo] See **Mucho**.

Murúm [mu’ruŋ] *adj* (*<M. murong*)
1. Depressed.
2. Taciturn.
3. Sad. *Cavâ uví nova, já ficâ murúm* he was saddened by the news.

Musiquêro [musi’kẹro] *n*
Musician. See **Tuna, *tuna di musiquêro***.

Muto [‘mutu] *adv*
Many.
Muto tánto [‘mutu ‘tąntu] very many.

Nâ^{1} [nạ] *excl* (<*M. nyah*)
Emphatic particle. *Cudí ná!* help! *Vai racolê nâ!* go away! *Vai-nâ, mufino!* get lost, you idiot!

Nâ^{2} [nạ] *adv*
Still, yet. *Já cavâ fazê liçám di casa? Nunca na, falta três folia* have you finished your homework yet? not yet, I still have three pages.
Ela tâ assí chistosa na? certo, iou-sa Marichai dia-a-dia tâ más bunita she still looks so pretty, doesn't she? Of course, Marichai gets prettier by the day.

Na^{3} [nạ] *neg*
Negative particle that is only used in the expression **na-más**.

Ná^{4} [nạ] *excl* (<*C. la*^{4} 嗱)
Here it is.

Na^{5} [na] *prep*
1. to.
2. in.

Nacê^{1} [na'sẹ] *vi*
To be born. *Quiança já nacê* the baby was born.

Nacê^{2} [na'sẹ] *vt*
To give birth. *Beba já nacê quiança* Beba had a baby.

Náchi ['nạči] *n*
Chinese, *syn* **China**. *Quelê-tánto náchi-náchi na festa* there were a lot of Chinese at the party.

Nadâ [nạ'dạ] *vi*
To swim.

Nádi ['nạdi] *fut-irr neg part*
Particle expressing negative future tense. *Êle nádi vai* he will not go. *Nós nádi falâ* we will not say anything. *Iou sâm nádi vai!* I am sure not going!

Nâm [nạŋ] See **Nôm**.

Nairo ['nạiru] *n*
Japanese seaperch (*Lateolabrax japonicus*).

Nairo-fogo [nąiru'fọgo] *n*
Barramundi (*Lates calcarifer*).

Na-más [nąʻmąs] *adv*
1. No more.
2. Only.
Dós na-más only two.

Nancassá [naŋka'sa] See **Nuncassá**.

Nariz [nąʼris] *n*
Nose. *Nariz chapado* flat nose. ***Nariz comprido*** [nąʼris kum'pridu] somebody who can sniff out what is happening.

Nê-bôm [nẹ'bọŋ] *adv neg*
It's not good, better not. *Nê-bôm cabeçudo* don't be stubborn. *Nê-bôm medo* don't be afraid.

Nele [ʻnẹli] *n* (<*Dr. nellu*)
1. Brown rice.
2. Rice husk.

Neto [ʻnẹtọ] *n*
Grandson. *Neto-neto* grandchildren.

Nhamada [ɲąʼmąda] *n*
Yam preserve.

Nhame [ʻɲami] *n*
Yam (*Dioscorea batata*).
Nhame chicú See **Chicú**.

Nhi [ɲi] See **Nhim**.

Nhim [ɲiŋ], **nhi** [ɲi] *n*
1. Girl.
2. Formal address for young girls, single women and lowly women of a certain age.

Nhinina [ɲiʼnina] *n*
Diminutive of **nina**.

Nhom [ɲoŋ] See **Nhum**.

Nhônha [ʻɲọɲa] *n*
Girl, young married or single woman.
Nhonhônha abbreviated form

of *nhônha-nhônha* women, ladies.

❖***Língua nhônha*** ['liɲgwa 'ɲọɲa] old creole of Macao.

Nhum [ɲuŋ], **nhom** [ɲoŋ] *n*

Boy, young man of modest status.

Nhunhum men, gentlemen.

Nim [niŋ] *conj*

Nor, neither.

Nina ['nina] *n*

1. Young girl, girl.
2. Single girl.

Ninguim [niŋ'giŋ] *pron*

Nobody.

Nôm [nọŋ], **nâm** [nạŋ] *adv*

Not, negative commonly used in declarative phrases in the present tense. *Ilôtro nôm têm vegónha êles* they are not ashamed.

Nôm têm nada [nọŋ tẹŋ 'nąda] (i) nothing special; (ii) it's not important; (iii) no problem; you're welcome.

Nomestê [nomẹs'tẹ] See **Mestê**.

Nómi ['nọmi] *n*

Name.

❖ ***Nómi di casa*** ['nọmi di 'kaza], or ***nómi dóci*** ['nọmi'dọsi] pet name, diminutive, affectionate family name: *Ato, Bútchi, Caco, Dim-dim, Chai-chai, Nano, Nini, Meno, Mimi, Nené.*

Nono ['nọno], **nuno** ['nuno] *n*

Transparent, fine cotton cloth.

Novémbro [no'vembru] *n*

November.

Novilêro [nọvi'lẹro] See **Nuviléro**.

Nunca ['nuŋka] *part neg*

No, negation commonly used in the past tense. *Êle nunca vêm* he never came.

Nunca-si [ʻnuŋkasi] never. *Êle nunca-si vêm* he never came.

Nuncassá [nuŋka'sa], **nancassá** [naŋka'sa] *vm neg*
It's not necessary. *syn* **Nomestê**. *Nancassá corê* there's no need to run. *Nancassá cerimónia* don't make a fuss. *Nancassá inventâ* don't lie.

Nuviléro [nuvi'lęro], **novilêro** [nọvi'lẹro] *adj*
1. Somebody who likes to spread news.
2. Troublemaker.

Ô [ọ] *disj*

Or. *Vôs tâ uví, ô tâ finzí surdo?* are you listening or pretending to be deaf.

Obrâ [ọ'brạ] *vi*

To defecate.

Obrea [o'brẹa] *n*

1. Host.
2. Wafer.

Oficina [ofi'sina] *n*

1. Office.
2. Department.
3. Factory.

Ôclo ['ọclu] *n*

Spectacles.

Olâ [ọ'lạ] *vt*

1. To see. *Vôs olâ!* Veja lá! *Já olâ?* did you see? did you understand? *Olâ bêm-fêto!* look at that!

2. To look.

Olâ olâ sabe [ọ'lạ ọ'lạ 'sąbi] one look's enough.

Óla ['ọla] *n*

Palm leaf, used for wickerwork.

Ôlo ['ọlu] *n*

1. Eye, eyes.

Ôlo batê-batê ['ọlu ba'tẹ ba'tẹ] to blink quickly.

Ôlo cacai ['ọlu kạ'kại] ou ***ôlo enfiado*** ['ọlu infi'ądu] cross-eyed.

Ôlo fino [ọlu 'finu] slit eyes.

Ôlo di gaviám ['ọlu di gavi'aŋ] lively eyes.

Ôlo sentado ['ọlu sen'tądu] still gaze.

❖ ***Comê qui ficâ ôlo sentado*** [kọ'mẹ ki fi'kạ 'ọlu sẹn'tadu] to overeat, to stuff onself.

Ôlo empatucado ['ọlu impatu'kądu] goggly eyes.

Ôlo galado ['ọlu ga'lądu] somebody's whose sight has been bewitched, shining eyes.

Ôlo más grándi qui bariga ['ọlu mąz 'grandi ki bą'riga] eyes bigger than one's belly.

2. Shoot of a plant or tree. *Ôlo*

bambú bamboo shoot. *Ôlo de figuêra* banana palm shoot.

Ôlo-deco [ˈọlu ˈdẹku] *n* (<*P. olho + de + cú*)
Anus.

Onçóm [ọnˈsọŋ], **unçôm** [uŋˈsọŋ], **ungsóm** [uŋˈsọŋ], **unsóm** [unˈsọŋ] *adv*
1. Alone, unaccompanied. *Êle onçóm vêm* he came alone. *Já ficâ onçóm* he was left alone.
2. Own, oneself. *Têm na onçóm sa casa* he is in his own home. *Sâm êle onçóm falâ* he says it himself.

Onde-onde [ˈọndi ˈọnde] *n* (<*M. ondeh*)
Small cake made of rice flour, filled with raw sugar and coconut.

Ông [ọŋ] *n* (<*C. aang*[6] 甖)
Clay barrel.

Onte [ˈọnti] *adv*
Yesterday.

Onte-onte [ọntiˈọnti], ***antezónte*** [anteˈzọnti] day before yesterday

Onzeletra [ọŋzeˈlẹtra] *adj*
1. Telltale.
2. Troublemaker.

Ora [ˈọra] *n*
1. Hour.
2. Occasion, time. *Ora-ora* occasions, times. *Desde qui ora?* for how long? *Têm ora* (i) there are times; (ii) sometimes. *Chegâ ora* at the right time, when the time is right.

Orde [ˈọrdi] *n*
Order. *Seguí orde* to follow orders. *Orde têm na rabo* to ignore an order.

Orelha-di-rato [oˈrẹλa di ˈrạtu] *n*
Black fungus which looks like rats' ears after cooking, called <*wan*[4] *yi*[2] 雲耳> in Chinese.

Oteu [ọ’tẹu] *n*
Metal instrument for prying oysters off rocks.

Otróra [ọ’trọra] *adv*
Long ago, formerly.

Otrung’a [ọ’truŋa] *quant*
Other, another. *Otrung’a dia* the other day. *Otrung’a vánda* the other side. *Sâm otrung’a* it’s another.

Otubro [ọ’tubru], [ọ’trubu] *n*
October.

Ova d’aranha [‘ọva da’rạɲa] *n*
Macanese cake which is hollow and very light.

Ovo-pôdre [‘ọvo ’pọdre] *n*
“Thousand year” egg, hen’s egg covered in a muddy paste and rice husks, **nele**, and preserved until it becomes black and gelatinous. Called <*pei*^{4} *tan*^{2} 皮 蛋> in Chinese.

Ovo prêto [ọvo’prẹtu] *syn* **Ovo pôdre**.

Ovo salgado [ọvo sal’gadu] *n*
Duck egg salted raw in its shell. Called <*hám*^{4} *tán*^{2}咸蛋> in Chinese.

Pa [pa], **Pra** [pra] *prep*
1. To.
2. For. *Passâ iou pa mentiroso* to take me for a liar.

Pacapiu [pąką'piw] *n* (<*C. pak⁹ kap³ piu¹* 白鴿票)
Chinese lottery.

Pachacha [pa'čąča] *n*
Vulva.

Paché [pa'čę] *n*
1. Parasol. *Na básso di sól fórti amestê abrí paché* under the hot sun it's necessary to use an umbrella.
2. Umbrella.

Pac-co-chôc [pą kọ'čọ] *n* (<*C. pa⁹ ko² tsok⁷* 白果粥)
Plain congee.

Pacfanista [pąkfa'nista] *n* (<*C. pak⁹ fan²* 白粉 + *P. -ista*)
Drug addict (heroine or cocaine).

Paço ['pąsu] *n*
Rough clay vessel; vase, basin, chamber pot.
Paço-buiám ['pąsu bui'aŋ] fragile rough clay pot. ***Paço-dente*** ['pąsu 'dęnti] large clay bowl scored inside and used formerly by Macanese housewives to grind the shrimps for **balichám**, grate coconut, wash rice, etc.

Paga ['pąga] *n*
Salary, wages. *Quelóra recebê paga* when I get paid. *Êle têm bôm paga* he has a good salary.

Pagode [pą'gọdi] *n*
Chinese Buddhist temple.

Pai-avô [pai a'vọ] *n*
Grandfather.

Pai-cun [pai'kun] *n* (<*C. pai⁴ cun²* 牌館)
Gambling den.

Pai-kâu [pąi'kąw] *n* (<*C. pai⁴ kau²* 牌九)
A kind of gambling game, similar to dominos.

Pai-mai [pại'mại] *n*
1. Parents.
2. Mother and father.

Pala ['pala] *n*
1. Effort.
2. Connection. *Têm ajuda di pala fórti* to be helped by an influential person.

Palancha [pa'laɲča] *n*
Scaffold, bamboo structure erected by Chinese builders, now less commonly used due to steel frames. *Marâ palancha* to tie or put up scaffolding.

Palangana [palaŋ'gạna] *n*
Oblong dish or platter for serving food at table. *Palangana grándi-grándi di sôm* large platter of food.

Palám-palám [pa'laŋ pa'laŋ] *adv*
(<*M. palang, pelangah*)
Completely, all. *Abrí janela palám-palám* to throw the windows wide open.

Palánqui [pą'laŋki], **palanquim** [palaŋ'kiŋ] *n*
Sedan chair, formerly used in Macao, with the passenger carried in a compartment balanced between two coolies. *syn* **Cadéra**.

Palavrám [pala'vraŋ] *n*
1. Obscenity. *Respondê co palavrám* to respond by swearing.
2. Unusual word.

Palestrâ [palẹs'trạ] *vi*
1. To lecture.
2. To chat.

Palpâ [pal'pạ] *vt*
To feel. *Palpâ pulso* (i) to feel a pulse; (ii) to get the measure of somebody, to feel somebody out.

Pâm [pạŋ] *n*
1. Bread.
Pâm-di-casa [pạŋ di 'kąza] very light, sweet bread, usually made at home.

❖ ***Nôvo-nôvo, pâm co ovo*** [ˈnọvu ˈnọvu pạŋ ko ˈọvo] the new brush sweeps clean.
2. Small piece of any substance.

Pancá [pạŋˈkạ] *n* (<*Hin. Pankha‹*) Punkah, large fan made of canvas attached to the ceiling and swung by hand, no longer used given the development of electric fans and air conditioning.

Pancada [paŋˈkạda] *n*
1. Blow, hit. *syn* **Cúti**.
2. Jiffy. *Ung'a pancada já fazê tudo ancusa* he did everything in a jiffy.

Pancho [ˈpạɲču] *adj & n* Idiot, fool.

Pandegâ [pandęˈgạ] *vi* To make merry, engage in boisterous festivities.

Panela [paˈnęla] *n* Hymen. *Tirâ panela* to deflower.

Pangalhada [paŋgaˈʎada] *n* Commotion.

Panhâ [paˈɲạ] *vi & vt*
1. To get. *Panhâ chapêu cubrí* to grab a hat. *Já panhâ subissalto* he got a fright. *Panhâ carôlo qui fundâ miolo* to get a huge thwack, a big hiding.
2. To gather.
3. To hit the mark. *Já panhâ* it's a strike!

Panha [ˈpạɲa] *n* Very fine, silky cotton made from the seeds of the silk cotton tree (*Bombax malabaricum*).

Páno [ˈpạnu] *n* Cloth. Any linen or cotton cloth.
❖ ***Páno elefánti*** [ˈpạnu eleˈfạnti] white cloth used for sheets. <Elefante> was formerly a popular brand.
❖ ***Páno-manila*** [ˈpạnu maˈnila] brightly striped or

checked cotton formerly manufactured in Manila.

Pantominéro [pantomi'nęro] *n*
Fraudster, swindler, cheat.

Papa-Cantám ['pąpa kan'taŋ] *n*
Mumps.

Papa-papa ['pąpa 'pąpa] *adj*
Soggy.

Papelazi [pape'lązi] *n*
Pile of papers.

Papel-pagode [pa'pęl pą'gǫdi] *n*
Very cheap absorbent paper, formerly used by poor people as toilet paper. Called <*chou*^{2} *chi*^{2} 草紙> in Chinese.

Papel-vento [pa'pęl 'vẹntu] *n*
Very fine but strong paper used formerly by Macanese confectioners to spread out dough. Called <*sa*^{1} *chi*^{2} 紗紙> in Chinese.

Pápi ['pąpi] *n*
Daddy.

Papiâ [pąpi'ạ] *vi*
1. To chat, talk.
2. To speak, say. *Papiâ bêm-fêto* to speak well.
Qui cuza vôs tâ papiâ? What are you saying?
3. To speak **patuá**. *Papiâ nôsso língu* to speak our language.
Papiâ vento [pąpi'ạ 'vẹntu] to talk nonsense, non sequiturs.

Papiaçám [pąpia'saŋ] *n*
1. Talk, conversation. *Um-cento papiaçám* lots of talk.
2. To speak. *Sâm nosso papiaçám* it's our way of speaking.
See **Patuá**.

Papito [pa'pitu] *n* (<*P. palpite*)
Premonition.

Parabiça [para'bisa] *n*
1. Nonsense, absurdity.
2. Incoherence.

Parám [pą'raŋ] *n* (<*M. parang*)
Cleaver, large kitchen knife normally used in Macao.

Paramentâ [pąramen'tą] *vi*
To dress up, get dressed up to the nines.

Parcâ [pąr'ką] *vt* (<*Eng. park*)
To park a vehicle.

Parcage [par'kaži] *n*
Parking for a vehicle.

Pasquim [pąs'kiŋ] *n*
Newspaper.

Passâ [pą'są]
To pass. *Passâ pa dôdo* to pass as crazy.
Passâ vale to sign a credit note.
Passâ casa [pą'są 'kaza] to move house.
Passâ fora! [pą'są 'fǫra] go away!

Passiâ [pą'sią] *vi*
Passear.
Passiâ-rua [pąsi'a 'rua] To go for a walk.

Pastro ['pąstru] *n*
Bird. *Home di caçâ pastro* bird-catcher. **Ninho di pastro** ['niɲǫ di 'pastrǫ] (i) nest; (ii) swallow's nest, which forms the basis for bird's nest soup.

Pataca [pa'tąka] *n*
Macao's currency. The pataca is divided into *avos*.

Patachoca [pata'čǫka] *n*
1. Sluggish woman.
2. Insipid person.

Pateca [pa'tęka] *n*
Watermelon.

Patinga [pa'tiŋga] *n* (<*Kon./Mar. pāti*)
Calf (leg).

Patôco [pa'tǫko] *n*
1. Boil.
2. A bump on the head. *Já cai, sai patôco na cabeça* he fell and bumped his head.

Patoá [pątu'ą] See **Patuá**.

Patuá [pątu'ą] *n* (<*Fr. patois*)
Macao's Creole language, also called **maquista**, **língua nhom**, **língua nhônha**, and **papiaçám**.

Patuscada [patus'kąda] *n*
Large meal, big spread.

Pau [pąw] *n*
1. Wood. *Pau sibocau* sappan-wood (*Caesalpinia sapan*).
2. Chinese measure of length, equivalent to around 36 cm.

Pauchong [paw'čǫŋ] *n* (<*C. pau^3 cheong^2 炮仗*)
Firecracker.

Pê [pẹ] *n*
Feet.
❖ ***Pê di piano*** [pẹ di pi'ạnu] thick feet, like those of a piano.
Pê marado [pẹ ma'rądu] small feet, like those of a goat.
Pê solto [pẹ 'sọltu] unbound feet, the opposite of **pê marado**.

Pedente [pędẹnti] *adj*
Annoying, insistent (begging).

Pedí [pę'di] *vt*
To ask. *Pedí sapeca pa caxa* to ask for a tip.
Pedí entrada [pę'di in'trąda] to request permission from a girlfriend's parents to visit her at home.

Pêdo [pẹdu] *n*
Fart.

Pêdo-di-Adám ['pẹdu di a'daŋ] *n*
Youngest child, kid, scamp.

Pedra-tafú ['pędra tą'fu] *n*
Kind of chalk powder that is used in preparing **taufú**.

Pedrume [pe'drumi] *n*
Alum, formerly used in home remedies, especially for headaches.

Pegâ [pę'gạ] *vt*
To hold. *Pegâ sono* to nod off, fall asleep.

Pegâ mám andâ [pę’gạ maŋ an’dạ] to walk hand in hand.

Pêle [‘pẹli] *n*

Skin.

❖ ***Pêle-fino*** [‘pẹli ’finu] used to describe a hypersensitive or touchy person.

❖ ***Pêle-grôsso*** [‘pẹli ’grọso] somebody who is thick-skinned, shameless.

Pê-mám [pẹ‘maŋ] See **mám**, **cai pê-mám**.

Pendurâ [pendu’rạ] *vt*

To hang.

❖ ***Pendurâ tacho*** [pendu’rạ ‘tąčọ] to have not enough money to buy food.

❖ ***Pendurâ quinzana na prêgo*** [pendu’rạ kin’zana na ‘prẹgu] to pawn the clothes off one’s back.

Penicâ [pini‘kạ] *vi*

To excel.

Pensám [pen‘saŋ] *n*

1. Worry, care. *Iou qui pensám* I was very worried. *Nunca assí pensám* don’t worry.

2. Retirement pension. *Êle tâ comê pensám* he’s retired, drawing his pension.

3. Small hotel.

Perada [pę’rąda] *n*

Hard throw of a ball. *Já levâ ung’a perada na cara qui ficâ vangueado* the ball hit him so hard in the face that he fainted.

Perdê [per’dẹ] *vt*

To lose.

Perdê chávi [per’dẹ ‘čąvi] to have diarrhoea.

Perna [‘pęrna] *n*

Upper part of the leg.

Perna grande [‘pęrna ’grąndi] thigh.

❖***Perna azêdo*** [‘pęrna a’zedu] used when (i) the leg muscles ache; (ii) the legs are weak.

Perto [‘pȩrtu] *adv*

1. Near, next. *Perto di Macau* near Macao. *Perto-perto* very near.

2. Almost. *Perto fêto* almost done.

Pesépio [pi’zȩpiu] *n*

Nativity scene.

Péscu [‘pȩsku] *n*

Peach. *Arve di péscu* peach tree.

Pê solto [pȩ ’sǫltu] See **Pê**, **Chipim**.

Péssa [‘pȩsa] *adv*

Quickly. *Péssa vai* go quickly. ***Péssa-péssa*** [‘pȩsa ‘pȩsa] in a hurry.

Pêsse [‘pȩsȩ], **pêxe** [‘pȩsšȩ] *n*

Fish. *Pêsse-cucús* steamed fish. *Pêsse-cabús* small fish commonly found at the riverbank, possible goby (*Gobioides*).

Petoral [pȩto’rąl] *adj*

Decongestant, for the chest or lungs.

Pichote [pi’čǫti], [pi’šǫti] *adj & n*

1. Small, short person.

2. Brat, scamp, kid.

Pico [‘piku] *n*

Picul, weight equivalent to 100 catties. See **Cate**.

Pilâ [pi’lạ] *vt*

1. To pound with a pestle.

2. To massage using a fist pounding lightly on the back like a pestle. *Pilâ costa* to massage in this manner.

Pilám [pi’laŋ] *n*

Pestle.

Pilizâ [pili’zạ] *vt*

1. To question, dispute, fight.

2. To become angry.

Pilizaina [pili’ząina] *n*

Major argument. *Grándi*

pilizaina na casa domestic strife.

Pilizám [pili'zaŋ] *n*
Quarrelsome, rowdy.

Pilizóna [pili'zona] *n*
Row, commotion.

Pilóló [pilǫ'lǫ] *n*
Penis. *syn* **Pirilau**.

Pimpám [pim'paŋ] *n*
Boaster, braggart.

Pinchâ [piŋ'ča̢] *vt*
1. To fling, throw. *Pinchâ iou na ung'a canto* he threw me into a corner. *Pinchâ fora* to throw away.
2. To squander.

Pinga[1] ['piŋga] *n*
Drop (of liquid).

Pinga[2] ['piŋga] *n (<M. punggah)*
1. Rod for carrying sedan chair, balanced on the shoulders.
2. Rod for carrying a coffin.
3. Bamboo rod that Chinese workers and traders use to hang their tools or wares.
4. Portion of water that Chinese water-carriers used to carry in two tins hanging from the **pinga**.

Pingâ [piŋ'ga̢] *vi*
To drip. *Pingâ-pingâ a*os pingos.
❖***Pingâ babo*** [piŋ'ga̢ 'ba̢bu] to be overcome with envy.

Pintura [pin'tura] *n*
1. Print, picture.
2. Picture on playing cards.
3. Photograph. *Tirâ pintura* to take a photograph.
4. Film. *Olâ pintura* to watch a film.

Pió [pi'ǫ] *adj*
Worse. *Pió qui êle, nunca olâ* I've never seen anything worse than him.

Pipis [pi'pis] *n* (<*M. pipis*)
Kind of cake mentioned in 19th century folk songs.

Piquinino [piki'ninu] *adj*
Small, very small.

Píqui-píqui ['piki 'piki] *n*
1. Polka dots. *Saia di pano píqui-píqui* polka dot skirt. *Sai sarampo, fica cara inchido di píqui-píqui* he caught measles and his face was covered with spots.
2. Splashes. *Já saltâ píqui-píqui di téra na rópa* her dress was splashed with mud.

Pirilau [piri'lạu] *n*
Penis.

Pisco ['pisku] *adj*
Cross-eyed.

Pisente [pi'zẹnti] *n*
Present, gift.

Pisidénte [pizi'dẹnti] *n*
President.

Pispóti [pis'pọti] *n*
Chamber-pot, spittoon.

Pitâ [pi'tạ] *vi*
To escape, flee. *Pitâ aula* to sneak away from class.

Pitada [pi'tada] *n*
Escapade, flight.

Pití-potóc [pi'ti pọ'tọk|] a*dj & n*
1. Timid, fearful. *Vôs qui arviro, fazê iou pití-potóc* you're left me in a real pickle, you scamp.
2. Weakling, person who falls sick easily.

Pitis [pi'tis] *n*
Very little, just a bit.

Pitisquéra [pitis'kẹra] *n*
Delicacy.

Pivête [pi'vẹti] *n*
Joss stick burned by Chinese at prayer. *Pivête cera* wax incense.

Pô! [pọ] See **Pôssa!**, **Pôfa!**

Pó-brânco [pọ 'brạŋku] *n*
1. Heroine.
2. Cocaine.
(*Cfr. C. pak⁹ fan² 白粉*)

Pobre-limpado ['pọbri lim'pądu], **pobre-cú-limpado** ['pọbri ku lim'pądu] *n*
Poor person, a nobody.

Pochopóc [počo'pọk|] *n*
Onomatopoeic word. Noise when somebody falls.

Pôfa! ['pọfa], **Pô!** [pọ] *interj*
Expression of disappointment, disillusion.

Pomo ['pọmo] *n*
Apple.

Póng-chán ['pọŋ čạn] *vt* (<*C. pong¹ chan³ 幫襯*)
To give business, be a customer.

Pontâ [pọn'tạ] *vt*
1. To aim.
2. To hit.

Pontapê [ponta'pẹ] *n*
To kick.
Já dâ ung'a pontapê na siara
[ǰa dạ 'uŋa ponta'pẹ na 'syara]
fig he left his wife.

Pónti ['pọnti] *n*
Bridge.

Pônto ['pọntu] *n*
Tenth part of a Chinese inch, the units into which the Chinese foot is divided. See also **Pau**.

Pônto-sorte ['pọntu 'sọrti] *n*
A Chinese martial art.

Popâ [pọ'pạ] *vt*
To save, economise.

Porcelana [porse'lạna], **porçolana** [porso'lạna] *n*
Ceramic bowl. *Já comê dôs porcelana di arôz* he ate two bowls of rice.
See also **Vun**.

Porco [‘pǫrku] *n*
1. Pig.
2. Pork.
Porco balichám tamarinho [‘pǫrku bali’čaŋ tama’riɲo] Macanese dish prepared with pork, tamarind and the traditional dried shrimp paste, **balichám**.
Porco chau-chau parida tamarinho [‘pǫrku čąw čąw pa’rida] special pork stew served to woman after giving birth.

Porquéro [por’kęro] *n*
Pig farmer.

Porta [‘pǫrta] *n*
Door.
Porta-casa [‘pǫrta ’kąza] door to the street, front door.
Porta-trás [‘pǫrta trąs] back door.

Portuguesado [portuge’ządu] *adj*
Portuguese-style. *Falâ portuguesado* to speak (Portuguese) in the Portuguese way, and not in the **patuá** style.
See **Torâ português**.

Pôssa! [‘pọsa], **Pô!** [pọ] *interj*
Phew! An expression of relief.

Postâ [pọs’tą] *vt* (<*Eng. post*)
To send a letter.

Potóm [pọ’tọm] See **Lorcha-potóm**.

Pramicedo [prami’sẹdu] *adv*
Early in the morning.

Pramor di [pra’mọ di] *adv & conj*
Because of. *Pramor di nosso pecado* because of our sins.

Prêgo [‘prẹgu] *n*
Pawnshop.
Chapâ prêgo [čą’pą ‘prẹgo] to pawn.

Prendê [pren’dẹ] *vt*
1. To arrest. *Puliça prendê êle* the policeman arrested him.

2. To learn. *Maria tâ prendê cuzinhâ* Maria is learning to cook.

Presiána [presi'ạna] *n*
Window blinds.

Prestada [pres'tạda] *adj*
Talented girl or woman, skilled at housework.

Priguntâ [prigun'tạ] *vt*
To ask.

Provetâ [prove'tạ] *vt*
To profit, take advantage of, make good use of.

Púfis! ['pufis] interj
See **Pofa**!

Puliça [pu'lisa] *n*
Policeman.
Puliça-môro [pu'lisa 'mọru] Indian soldier formerly recruited from Goa, Damao and Diu to serve in Macao's police force.
Puliça pau [pu'lisa pạw] policeman (who used to carry a wooden truncheon).
See also **Chanquêm**.

Pulú [pu'lu] *n* (<*M. pulut*)
Glutinous rice.

Pum [puŋ] *n*
Fart.

Pussâ [pu'sạ] *vt*
To pull.
Pussâ âncora subí bafado [pu'sạ aŋ'kora su'bi ba'fạdu] to lift anchor.
Pussâ bafado [pu'sạ ba'fạdu] (i) to pant; (ii) tired, out of breath.
Pussâ beço [pu'sạ 'bẹ'su] to show displeasure, turning down one's mouth.
Pussâ caréta [pu'sạ ka'rẹta] to pull a rickshaw.
Pussâ comprido [pu'sạ kum'pridu] to prolong, extend.
Pussâ ôlo [pu'sạ 'ọlu] to attract attention.

Putau [pu'tạw] *n* (<*C. put*[8] *tau*[4] 鉢頭)

Rough, round shallow clay dish used in the kitchen.

❖ ***Cai na putau*** [kại na pu'tạw] to blunder.

❖ ***Cara di putau*** ['kąra di pu'tạw] stupid-looking, cretin.

Quachí [kwą'či] *n* (<*C. kua*[1] *chi*[2] 瓜子)
Seeds, watermelon seeds.

Qualung'a [kwą'luŋa] *pro interrog*
Which.

Quarénta [kwa'ręnta] *num*
Forty. *Quarénta-fora* forty odd.

Quarentóra [kwaren'tǫra] *n*
Revelry, Carnival.

Quartinho-banho [kwar'tiɲu 'baɲu] *n*
Bathroom.

Quebrâ [kę'brą] *vt*
To break, split.
Quebrâ cabeça [kę'brą ka'bęsa] (i) to dwell on something; (ii) to try to solve a problem.
Quebrâ sono [kę'brą 'sǫnu] (i) to disturb (somebody's) sleep; (ii) to wake up.

Quecido [kę'sidǫ], **crecido** [kre'sidu] *adj*
Grown up, developed.

Queique [keik] *n* (<*Eng. cake*)
Large, heavy spiced fruit cake soaked in brandy, usually served at Christmas and in general at all important Macanese parties.

Quelê[1] [kę'lę] *adj & pron*
1. Which.
2. That.

Quelê[2] [kę'lę] *det & pro*
Any.

Quelê-môdo [kę'lę 'mǫdo] *adv*
1. How, in what way. *Quelê-môdo lôgo têm* how will there be. *Quelê-môdo pôde falâ* how can it be said.
2. Anyhow. *Quelê-môdo tamêm sâm assí* any way is the same.

Quelê tánto [kę'lę 'tąntu] *adv*
1. Any amount. *Quelê tánto*

tamém iou lôgo comprâ I will buy however much there is.
2. Large quantity, a lot. *Quelê tánto gente já vêm* a lot of people came.

Quelóra [kẹ'lọra] *adv temp*
When, the moment when. *Quelóra largâ iou vêm fora* when you brought me into this world.
Quelóra iou já cai the instant I fell.

Quémbra ['kẹmbra] *n*
Cramp.

Quentâ [ken'tạ] *vt*
To warm, heat. *Quentâ comida* to warm up food.

Querê [kẹ'rẹ] *vt*
1. To want. *Qui-cuza vôs querê?* what do you want?
2. To love. *Iou muto querê pa vôs* I love you deeply.
3. To desire. *Sâm quim querê?* who wants it?

Quêro ['kẹro] Decreolisation, hyper-correction of the verb **querê**. Found in negative and interrogative phrases. *Êle nôm-quêro vai,* he does not want to go. *Vôs quêro nôm-quêro comprâ?* to you want to buy or not?

Qui [ki] *pron*
What, which.
Qui cuza? [ki 'kuza] what, what's that?
Qui laia [ki 'ląya] how, in what way?
Qui nova? ['ki 'nọva] how are you? what's new?
Qui pôde! ['ki 'pọde] to be able. *Vôs qui pôde* how can you!
Qui sabe! [ki 'sąbi] how should I know! who knows!
Qui-di ['kidi] where.
Qui-foi? [ki'fọi] why?
Qui aqui, qui ạlí [ki a'ki ki a'li] either here or there.

Quiada [ki'ąda] *n*
Maid.

Quiança [ki'ạŋsa] *n*
Child. *Quiança-quiança* children.

Quim [kiŋ] *pron*
Who. *Sâm quim?* who is it? *Sâm di quim?* whose is it? *Quim já vêm?* who came?

Quimâ [ki'mạ] *vt*
1. To burn.
2. To squander. *Quimâ sapeca* to waste money unnecessarily.

Quimám [ki'maŋ] *n* (<*J. kimono*)
Traditional Chinese lady's silk tunic.

Quinzéna [kin'zẹna], [kiŋ'zẹna] *n*
Man's coat.

Quirubim [kiru'biŋ] *n*
1. Cherub.
2. Spoiled child, doted on by the family.

Quivichi-quiváchi [ki'viči ki'vạči] *adj*
Babbling, unintelligible speech, tripping over one's words.

Rabám [rą'baŋ] *n*
Chinese man with queue, or pigtail (as seen in former days).

Raba-raba ['rąba 'rąba] *adj*
1. Common, rough. *Gente raba-raba* common people.
2. Poor quality. *Brêdo raba-raba* poor quality mix of vegetables.
3. Worthless.

Rabéca [ra'bęka] *n*
Fiddle, violin.

Rabiâ [rąbi'ạ] *vt*
To squint at, take a sideways glance.

Rabiadela [rąbia'dęla] *n*
Glimpse, glance.

Rabicâ [rąbi'kạ] *vi*
To put on heavy make-up. See also **Bacarâ**.

Rabichâ [rąbi'čạ] *vt*
1. To drag or pull somebody by the hair.
2. To drag somebody to go somewhere. *Já rabichâ iou sa juntado* you've already bent my ear to go with you.

Rabicho [rą'biču] *n*
Long braid that Chinese girls used to wear.

Rabiósque [rąbi'ǫski] *n*
Behind, buttocks.

Rabiscâ [rąbis'kạ] *vt*
To scribble, write.

Rabita [ra'bita] *n*
Young Chinese girls with braided hair.

Rabo-barata ['rąbu ba'rata] *n*
Dress coat, tails (Lit: <cockroach tail> *syn* **Tagalám**.

Rabo ['rąbu] *n*
Turnip.
Rabo-chapôi ['rąbu ča'pǫi] pickled turnip.

Rabucénga [rabu'sẹŋga], **rabucéng'a** [rabu'sẹŋa] *n*
1. Trifle, something inexpensive.
2. Bagatelle.
3. Various things.

Rabucéng'a [rabu'sẹŋa] See **Rabucénga**.

Rabujâ [rąbu'ǰạ] *vi & vt*
To scold, grumble.

Rabujento [rąbu'ǰẹntu] *n*
Grumpy person, somebody who is always scolding.

Rafundí [rafun'di] *n*
1. To put. *Iou nôm sabe úndi já rafundí iou-sua ôclo* I don't know where I put my glasses.
2. To hide. *Úndi ilôtro dôs já vai rafundí?* where did the pair of them hide?
3. To get lost. *Vai rafundí!* go on, get lost!

Rafêro [rą'fẹro] *adj*
1. Clumsy.
2. Useless.
3. Failure.

Ragaçâ [rąga'sạ] *vt*
To roll up, pull up. *Ragaçâ mánga* to roll up one's sleeves. *Ragaçâ saia, corê* to hoist up one's skirt and run.

Raganhado [rąga'ɲądo] *adj*
Grinning.

Ramatâ[1] [rąma'tạ] *vt* (<*P. rematar*)
To finish, conclude, end. *Fazê ramatâ* to finish something off, complete something. *Ramatâ vôs-sua estória* finish up your story.
Comê ramatâ [kọ'mẹ rąma'tạ] to eat everything.

Ramatâ[2] [rąma'tạ] *adv*
Also. *Já cunvidâ iou ramatâ* he ended up inviting me as well.

Ramêde [rą'mẹdi] *n*
1. Remedy, solution.
2. Fear, fright.
Qui ramêde! what can we do!

Ramela [rą'męla] *n*
Gummy secretion from the eye.
Ramelado [rąme'lądu] bleary. *Ôlo ramelado* bleary eyes.

Ramendâ[1] [rąmen'dą] *vt*
To seem (as if). *Êle ramendâ tâ reva* he seemed angry.

Ramendâ[2] [rąmen'dą] *adv*
Similar, just like. *Ramendâ ung'a porco* like a pig. *Ramendâ china-china* just like the Chinese.

Rancâ [rąn'ką] *vt*
To snatch. *Já rancâ di iou sua mám* it was snatched from my hands. *Vento di tufám já rancâ estung'a arvre* the typhoon uprooted this tree.
❖***Rancâ ôlo*** [rąn'ką 'ǫlu] to stare fearfully.

Ráncho ['raɲču] *n*
1. Soldier's mess.
2. Group. *Juntâ ráncho* to get together and form a group.

Rapaz-di-Diós [rą'pąs di 'diǫs] *n*
Expression of affection for boys.

Rapicâ [rąpi'ką] *vt*
To toll a bell.

Raspâ [rąs'pą] *vt*
To scrape.
Raspâ tacho [rąs'pą 'tąču] to scrape out the dish.
❖***Raspâ tripa*** [rąs'pą 'tripa] to try one last time for a child.

Raspiáti [rąspi'ąti] *n*
1. Pauper, poor but pretentious.
2. Poorly dressed.

Rato-di-sacristia ['rątu di sakris'tia] *adj & n*
Pious church-goer. *syn* **Biato-láp-chôk, bate-pêto**.

Ravirâ [rąvi'rą] *vt*
1. To turn round.
2. To run from one end to another.
3. To turn. *Ravirâ cabêça* to turn one's head.

❖ ***Comê qui ravirâ*** [kọ'mẹ ki rạvi'rạ] to stuff oneself.

Ravirado [ravi'rạdu] *adj*

1. Turned upside down.
2. Stretched, extended. *Torto-ravirado* stretched out.

Rê [rẹ] *n*

King. *Rê di festa* king of the party. *Têm rê na bariga, nôm pôde intrâ ung'a fijám* he who has a king in his stomach cannot make way for a bean, used to describe an arrogant person.

❖ ***Rê-di-bôlo*** [rẹ di 'bọlọ] spoilt child, rude child.

❖ ***Rê na bariga*** [rẹ na bạ'riga] boaster, cocky person, snob.

Recetâ [rẹsẹ'tạ] *vt*

To prescribe medicine.

Regra ['rẹgra] *n*

1. Line of writing. *Rabiscâ dôs regra* to write a couple of lines.
2. Rule, law, norm.

Remâ [rẹ'mạ] *vi*

1. To row.
2. To pick away at food with no appetite.

Renâ [rẹ'nạ] *vt*

To think, imagine. *Renâ maldade* to think of doing harm. *Sentâ na casa, renâ ancuza triste* to stay at home thinking of sad things.

Repente [re'pẹnti] *n*

Rush of bad temper.

Repimpado [repim'pạdu] *adj*

1. Comfortably settled.
2. Pampered.

Reportâ [repọr'tạ] *vt* (<*Eng. report*)

To report, denounce.

Respondéncia [respon'dẹnsia] *n*

Interest, yield. *Su sapeca têm respondéncia* your money yields interest.

Reva ['rẹva] *adj & vt*

Angry, annoyed. *Nê-bôm reva*

don't get angry. *Pai tâ reva* father is angry.

Rí [ri] *vi*
To laugh. *Rí qui istripâ* to split one's sides laughing.
Rí qui raganhâ to laugh one's head off.
Rí cacada to roar with laughter. *Nê-bôm fazê iou rí* don't make me laugh.

Risca ['riska] *n*
Stripe.
1. Row. *Risca di trás* back row.
2. Line.
3. Striped. *Rópa risca-risca* striped clothes.

Riscâ [ris'kạ] *vt*
1. To draw, mark.
2. To try one's luck in gambling.

Riva[1] ['riva] *n*
Top.

Riva[2] ['riva] *prep*
On top, above.

Rolâ [rǫ'lạ] *n*
1. To roll.
2. To roll up, to turn.
3. To mix.

Rompánte [rom'pạnti] *adj*
Proud, arrogant.

Roncâ [rǫŋ'kạ] *vi*
To snore.

Rónça-rónça ['rǫnsa 'rǫnsa] *vi*
1. Coming and going at a leisurely pace.
2. To drag.
3. To wander, stroll.

Rondade [ron'dadi] *n*
Malice.

Rondánte [ron'danti] *n*
1. Police patrol.
2. Policeman on duty at the police station.

Rópa ['rǫpa] *n*
1. Clothing. *Levâ rópa-rópa pa mainato* to take the washing to the laundry.
2. Dress.

❖ ***Rópa qui sai di bóca di cám*** [‘rǫpa ki sạị di ‘bǫka di kaŋ] wrinkled dress.
3. Suit.

Rósca-dóci [‘rǫska ‘dǫsi] *n*
Sweet bread in the form of a ring.

Rósca-melua [‘rǫska me’lua] *n*
Crescent-shaped sweet bread.

Rota [‘rǫta] *n* (<*M. rotang*)
1. Rattan, flexible cane for making walking sticks and canes.
2. Rattan walking stick.
3. Rattan cane.

Rotada [rọ’tąda] *n*
A caning.

Ruçâ [ru’sạ] *vt*
1. To scrub.
2. To scratch. *Ruçâ na parede* to scratch against the wall.
3. To rub in medicine. *Ruçâ quembra* to rub in medicine to cure cramp.

Rufâ [ru’fạ] *vt*
To eat with enjoyment.

Rúfa [‘rufa] *n*
Pataca; value in money. *Dez rúfa di van-tân* ten patacas of dumplings <*van*[4] *tan*[1] 餛飩 or 云吞>.

Rumâ [ru’mạ] *vt*
To tidy up. *Ruma livro na armário,* tidy up the bookshelves.

Rutiâ [ruti’ạ] *vt*
To beat with a cane. *Pegâ róta rutiâ di bêm* to grab a cane and administer it effectively.

Sa[1] [sa], **sua** [‘sua], **su** [su] *pron*
General possessive pronoun, functioning much as the English <’s>. *Iou-sa filo* my child. *Ilôtro-sa casa* their home.

Sa[2] [sa] adv
Expletive particle expressing confirmation or explanation. **Sâm diabo? Nunca, Sâm tacho-sa!**, is it **diabo**? No, it’s **tacho**.

Sá [są] See **Sabe**.

Sabe [‘sąbi], **sá** [są] *vt*
To know. *Cuza vôs sabe?* what do you know? *Nôs sabe têm na úndi* we know where it is. *Qui sabe!* how should I know! *Iou nôm sá sâm quim* I don’t know who it is.

Sabichám [sabi’čaŋ] *n*
Know-all.

Sabola [sa’bọla] *n*
Onion.

Saco-gúnde [‘sąku ’gundi] *n*
Empty rice sack used for wiping feet or as a door-mat.

Safo [‘sąfu] *adj*
Safe.

Saguám [są’gwaŋ] *n*
Atrium, open courtyard inside a house.

Saguáti [są’gwąti] *adv* (*<Hin./Per.saughāt*)
Free.

Sai [sại] *vi*
To go out. *Quiada já sai,* the maid isn’t working here any more. *Sai di quim?* who does he/she look like? *Cedo-cedo sai di casa* he/she left home very young.
Sai bafo [sại ‘bąfu] to speak, begin to speak. *Nê-bôm sai bafo!* don’t say anything!

Saia [‘sąia] *n*
Skirt, petticoat.

Saia-dentro [sąia 'dẹntru] lady's combinations.
Saia-cutám [sąia ku'taŋ] petticoat and camisole.
Saia froco-froco ['sąia 'froko 'froko] pleated skirt.

Saiám [say'aŋ] *adv* (<*M. sayang*)
1. What a pity. *Saiám vôs nôm pôde vêm* what a pity you can't come.
2. Nostalgia. *Churâ saiám Macau* to weep from missing Macao.

Saicó[1] [sąy'kọ] *n* (<*C. sai*³ *ko*³ *細個*)
1. Lad, urchin.
2. Message-boy working in an office, young gopher.
3. Scullion.

Saicó[2] [sąy'kọ] *adj* (<*C. sai*³ *ko*³ *細個*)
Small.

Saiong [sąi'ọŋ] *n* (<*C. sai*¹*yêng*⁴ *西洋*)
Portugal (*Lit.* <Western Ocean>).

Salcioso [sąlsi'ọsu] *adj*
Somebody who lisps.

Sâm [sąŋ] *v pred*
To be. *Iou sâm Macau-filo* I am from Macao.
Vôs sâm quim? who are you? *Sâm divera* it's true. *Macau sâm assí* that's how it is in Macao. *Nôs sâm gente bêm-fêto* we're serious people. *Ilôtro sâm aringuéra* they are tittle-tattlers.
Sâm nunca? [sąŋ 'nuŋka] *Lit.* isn't it? a question looking for confirmation, used at the end of an affirmative phrase. *Êle divera carajoso, sâm nunca?* he's really brave, isn't he?

Samatra [sa'mątra] *n*
Torrential downpour coinciding with a typhoon, leading to floods. Also called **samatrada**, or **águ di samatra**.

Samatrada [sama'trąda] See **Samatra**.

Sambal [sam'bạ l] *n* (<*M. sambal*)
Chutney made with mango, loquat, custard apple, onions and condiments served with some Macanese dishes.

Sám-lan-ché [sạm lan'čẹ] *n* (<*C. sam*^{1} *lon*^{4} *che*^{1} *三輪車*)
Tricycle (*Lit.* <three wheel car>), vehicle that originated in Malaysia and replaced the rickshaw in the late 1950s.

Sampán [sam'pán] *n* (<*C. san*^{1} *pan*^{2} *舢板*)
Small Chinese rowing boat.

San-chi-pai [san či'pại] *n* (<*C. san*^{1} *ju*^{2} *pai*^{3} *神主牌*)
Rectangular wooden plaque placed on a Chinese altar and bearing the name and place of birth of a deceased person.

Sanco ['sạŋku] *n* (<*M. sangku*)
Metal or ceramic bowl used as a spittoon or rubbish bin.

Sandê [san'dẹ] *vt*
To light. *Sandê candia* to switch on a light. *Sandê véla* to light a candle. *Sandê fôgo* to kindle a fire. *Sandê churuto* to light a cigar.

San Ma Lu [sạn mạ lu] *n* (<*C. san*^{1} *ma*^{2} *lou*^{6} *新馬路*)
Almeida Ribeiro Avenue in Macao, *Lit.* <new avenue >. Chinese name for the avenue, opened up following an urban overhaul in the early 20th century.

Sansám [saŋ'saŋ] *n*
Samson, strong man. *Fórti ramendâ sansám* as strong as Samson.

Santám [san'taŋ] *n* (<*M. santan*)
Coconut milk, used in various Macanese sweetmeats.

Santo ['sạntu] *n*
Image or statuette of a saint.

Sapám [sa'paŋ] *n* (<*M. sapang*)
Used in the expression **pau-**

sapám or sappanwood (*Caesalpinia sappan*) a chestnut red hard wood also called **pau-brasil**.

Sapeca [sa'pęka] *n*
1. Round copper coin, alloyed with tin or lead, with a square hole in the centre. Formerly used in China.
2. Money. *Iou nôm têm sapeca* I have no cash. *Êle têm tánto sapeca* he has a lot of money.
Sapeca fêmea [sa'pęka 'fęmia] easy money, money gained dishonestly.

Sarabanda [sąra'bąnda] *n*
Telling off, warning. *Já panhâ sarabanda* he got a telling off.

Saraça [sa'rąsa] *n* (<*M. sarasah*)
Colourful veil or mantilla with a printed design formerly worn by more ordinary Macanese women. Upper class women used a **dó**.

Saraçám [sara'saŋ] *n*
Mist.

Sarado [sa'rądu] *adj*
Half-open. *Porta sarado* door ajar.
Juízo sarado ['ǰwizu sa'rądu] narrow or miserly view of things.

Sarai-marai [sa'rąi ma'rąi] *adj* (<*M. serai*)
Repetitive. Usually used to describe older people.

Sarambau [saram'bąw] *n* (<*M. selambau*)
Fishing apparatus, with a net stretched between four bamboo rods, and formerly used along the sea wall. Called <*ngau[1] châng[1]* 拗罾> in Chinese.

Sarangông [sarąŋ'gǫŋ] *n* (<*M. sarang*)
Paper kite. *Largâ sarangông* (i) to fly paper kites; (ii) to play with paper kites.
❖***Rabo di sarangông*** ['rabu di sarąŋ'gǫŋ] used to describe somebody who follows others; committee.

Sarám-murúm [są'raŋ mu'ruŋ] *adj* (<*M. sarang* + *morong*) Dishevelled. *Cabelo sarám-murúm* tousled, uncombed hair.

Sarám-surave [sąraŋ su'rąvi] *n* (<*M. sarang* + *serabai*) Kind of Macanese cake.

Sará-sarú [sa'rą sa'ru] *adj & n* Somebody who drags his feet.

Sarneâ [sąrni'ą] *vt* To bother, annoy. *Passâ fora, na! Nê-bôm sarneâ iou* get lost, don't bother me!
❖ ***Sarna pa cuçâ*** ['sarna pa ku'są] troubles.

Salta-balada ['sąlta ba'ląda] *adj* Tomboy, very active.

Saván [są'vąn] *n* (<*M. sawan*)
1. Ailment caused by foul air, bad smells (for instance, of a dead rat, dirty drain, corpse), view of anything unpleasant, frightening, producing general malaise, loss of appetite, or a jinx.
2. According to tradition in Macao, the pernitious effect of ill airs on cakes and other baking which fails to rise, especially when a pregnant or menstruating woman is nearby.

Savanado [sava'nądu] *adj* Under the influence of **saván**. See also **Vantú**.

Seclo ['sęklu] *n* Century.
❖ ***Seclo seclórum*** ['sęklu se'klǫrum] (i) for a long time, for all eternity; (ii) something very old.

Sêco ['sẹku] *adj*
1. Dry.
2. Wilted.
Sêco ismirado ['sẹko zmi'rądu] (i) withered; (ii) parched.

Seguí [si'gi] *vt*
1. To follow.
2. To acompany. *Seguí trás* (i) to go behind; (ii) to acompany.

Seléa [se'lẹa] *adv*
Similar. *Selea asnéra* the same kind of foolery.

Senéfa [se'nęfa], **senéfra** [se'nęfra] *n*
Valance, pelmet.

Sentâ [sen'tạ] *vi & vt*
1. To sit down.
2. To be transported. *Sentâ caréta* to go by car. *Sentâ camiám* to take the bus.
3. To visit. *Quelóra têm tempo vêm sentâ* come and visit when you have time.
❖***Sentâ-sentâ*** [sen'tạ sen'tạ] no more, no less, just that.
❖***Comê qui sentâ ôlo*** [kọ'mẹ ki sen'tạ 'ọlu] to glut. Note: <ôlo> here refers to **ôlo décu**.

Sentí [sẹn'ti] See **Sintí**.

Seringatâ [siriŋga'tạ] *vi*
1. To nitpick.
2. To dabble, to stir up trouble.

Sevandizâ [sivandi'zạ] *vi*
To enjoy fully.

Sevandizo [sivan'dizu] *n*
Vermin.

Si [si] *conj*
If, depending upon. *Si sã capaz* if you are brave. *Si já falâ co iou* if you had told me. *Si vosôtro querê vêm* if you want to come. *Iou vai olâ si têm* I'm going to see if there is any.

Siara [sy'ara] *n*
1. Lady, Mrs.
2. Mother.
3. Housewife.
4. Wife. *Vôs-sa siara sâm bêm di astrevida* his wife is very feisty.

Siao [si'ąu] *n* (<*C. si⁶ iao⁴* 豉油) *syn* **Sutate**.

Siduzí [sidu'zi] *vt*
To captivate, enchant, seduce.

Sim[1] [siŋ] *adv aff*
Yes.

Sim[2] [siŋ] *prep*
Without. *Sim vegónha* shameless. *Já vai sim falâ co iou* he left without telling me. *Sim ninguim* alone.

Simpita [sim'pita] *n* (<*M. sumpitan*)
Bamboo pea-shooter used with beans or small stones.

Simpitâ [simpi'tạ] *vi & vt* (<*M. sumpit*)
To blow a bean out with a **simpita**.

Sinâ [si'nạ] *vt*
To sign.

Sin-pun [sin'pun] *n* (<*C. sun*[3] *pun*[4] 算盤)
Abacus. Manual calculator still frequently used by Chinese shopkeepers. *China dále sin-pun pa contâ más bêm-fêto* The Chinese man used his abacus to do the sum more accurately.

Siput [si'put] *n* (<*M. siput*)
Edible snail harvested from land along a watercourse.

Sintí [sin'ti], **sentí** [sẹn'ti] *vt*
1. To feel. *Sentí galánte* to feel out of place.
2. To find, think. *Sentí bôm* to think something is good. *Iou sintí qui vôs pôde vai* I think you can go.

Sisí[1] [si'si] *vi*
To urinate.

Sisí[2] [si'si] *n*
Urine.

Sissica [si'sika] *n*
Urine. *Fazê sissica* to urinate.

Sium [syuŋ] *n & trat*
1. Mr. *Sium Capitám* Captain, Sir.
2. Master.

Siviço [si'visọ] *n*
1. Service.
2. Work.

Sô [sọ] *adv*
Alone, only. See also **Sômente**.
Sô pa iou just for me.

Socâ [so'kạ] *vt*
1. To tie.
2. To tighten.
3. To splint.
4. *fig* To weave, intrigue. *Ai, qui socado!* oh, I was tricked!

Sôc-sôc [sọk'sọk] *n*
Armpit. Perspiration from the armpit. *Fêde sôc-sôc* smelling of sweat (from the armpit).

Sodado [sọ'dạdu] *n*
Soldier. *Sodado-sodado* soldiers. *Marchâ sodado* to march like soldiers.

Sôm[1] [sọŋ] *n (<C. sông*[3] *餸)*
Food. *Comprâ sôm* to do the marketing.
❖***Sôm-cachôro*** [sọŋ ka'čọro] dish made by using up odds and ends in the kitchen.
❖***Sôm di susto*** [sọŋ di 'sustu] improvised dish or dishes.

Sôm[2] [sọŋ], **sum** [suŋ] *n*
Sound. *Corneta nôm têm sôm* the horn has no sound.

Sombrêlo [som'brẹlo] *n*
1. Sunshade.
2. Umbrella.

Sômente [sọ'mẹnti] *adv*
Only, scarcely. *Sômente ung'a vez* just once. *syn* **Sô**.

Sonso ['sọnsọ], ['sọŋso] *adj*
1. Forgetful.
2. Careless.
3. Always distracted.

Sópa ['sọpa] *n*
Soup.
Sópa-sópa mulado ['sọpa·'sọpa mu'lạdu] drenched.
Sópa lacassá ['sọpa laka'sạ] vermicelli soup.

Sôr [sọr] *n*
Sweat. *Sôr pingado di testa* sweat dropping off one's forehead.

Sós [sọs] *n* (<*Eng. sauce*)
Sauce, usually of the Worcester variety.

Sossegâ [sose'gạ] *vi & vt*
To calm, pacify.

Su [su] See **Sa**.

Suâ [su'ạ] *vi & vt*
1. To sweat.
2. To bring on a sweat.
Suâ iou it makes me sweat.

Sua ['sua] See **Sa**.

Subí [su'bi] *vt*
To ascend. *Subí escada* to climb the stairs.
Subí génio [su'bi 'ǰẹnyu] to become enraged, become irritated.
Subí posto grándi [su'bi pọsto'grandi] to be promoted.

Subiâ [subi'ạ] *vi*
To whistle.

Subissalto [subi'sąlto] *n*
Fright, agitation.
Panhâ subissalto [pa'ɲạ subi'sąlto] to take fright.

Sucre ['sukre], ['sukri] *n*
Sugar. *Chá co sucre* sweet tea. *Dóci ramendâ sucre* dessert with sugar.
Sucre pedra ['sukri 'pẹdra] *açucar pedra,* raw sugar used in various Chinese desserts. Called <*pêng^1 tóng^4 冰糖*> in Chinese (*lit.* iced sugar).

Sugâ [su'gạ] *vt*
1. To wring.
2. To hang out the washing.
3. To dry.

Supiám [supi'aŋ] *n* (<*C. kóng^1 sou^1 péang^2 光酥餅*)
Whitish Chinese biscuit which is given to relatives and friends after a wedding feast or to

mark the first month of a baby's life.

Supo ['supo] *n* (<*Kon./Hin. sūp*)
Shallow, round basket used for steaming food in Chinese cuisine.

Suprâ [su'prạ] *vt*
1. To blow. *Suprâ vento di tufám* to blow in gusts of wind (as in a typhoon).
2. To inflate. *Suprâ balám* to inflate a balloon.

Suriada [suri'ąda] *n*
Large quantity, series. *Já sai ung'a suriada di pinta* a string of chickens was hatched. *Tâ sai quanto suriada di bolo bate pau* batches of mooncake are being made.

Suspendido [suspen'didu] *adj*
Suspended.

Susto ['sustu] *n*
Fright, fear. *Iou muto susto* I'm really afraid. *Fazê susto pa quiança* to scare a child.

Sutate [su'tąti] *n* (<*J. sutate*)
Soy sauce. *syn* **Siao**.
Cara di sutate ['kara di su'tąti] stupid-looking.

Suzâ [su'zạ] *vt*
To soil. *Suzâ chám* to dirty the floor.

Suzo[1] ['suzu] *adj*
Dirty.
❖***Cabeça suzo*** [ka'bęsa 'suzu] (i) suspicious person; (ii) person who is always thinking ill.

Suzo[2] ['suzu] *n*
Excrement. *Careta di suzo* cart that used to collect nightsoil. *Suzo barata* cockroach droppings. *Suzo di cachôro* dog excrement.

Tâ [ta] *part*
Indicates the aspect of the main verb. When the main verb conveys an action, **tâ** indicates an on-going action. When the main verb conveys a state, **tâ** indicates the current nature of this state. It can be used both in the past and the present tenses. *tâ lê* he is reading. *Iou tâ querê gritâ* I want to scream. *Iou tâ vai-ia* I'll be right there. *Acung'a quianca tâ churâ* that child is crying.

Tábu ['tąbu] *n*
Board. *Tábu di istricâ rópa* ironing board.

Tacada [ta'kąda] *n*
1. Blow, trick.
2. Way. *Buscâ ung'a tacada* to look for a way.
3. Astuteness.
Sã ung'a quiança inchido di tacada he is a very smart child.
4. Imagination. *Vôs nôm têm tacada* you have no imagination.
5. Instant. *Ung'a tacada já cavâ tudo* I got it done in a jiffy.

Tacanâ [tąka'nạ] *vi*
To steal, extract. *Já trepâ árvi pa tacanâ dôs carambola pa títi* he climbed the tree to steal to custard apples for his aunt.

Tachada [ta'čada], [ta'šada] *n*
1. Each batch of cakes ready to bake. *Títi já fazê sês tachada di alúa* aunty has made six batches of alua.
2. Drinking spree. *Tudo anôte-anôte panhâ tachada* he gets legless every night.

Ta-chim [ta'čiŋ], **dachim** [da'čiŋ] *n*
Chinese scales, usually held in one hand by a string attached to a calibrated rod with a dish hanging from one end and the relevant weight tied to the other end.

The large **ta-chim** is supported by two people on a rod (**pinga**) laid across their shoulders. These scales measure weights in catties (604 grams), piculs (100 catties), and taels (1/16 of a catty or 37.75 grams). *Ta-chim pesado* scales biased against the customer. *Êle-sua ta-chim bêm di pesado* the man is selling short.

Tacho [‘tąču] *n*
1. Bowl, frying-pan.
2. Name of a Macanese dish also called **chacháu pêle**.

Tafú [tą’fu] See **Taufú**.

Tafulâ [tąfu’lạ] See **Entafulâ**.

Tagalám [tąga’laŋ] *n*
Morning coat. *syn* **Rabo-di-barata**
Men’s formal coat.

Tai-mong [tai’mọŋ] *adj* (<*C. tai*^{6} *mong*^{2} 大懵)
Foolish; crazy.

Taipán [tại’pạn] *n* (<*C. tai*^{6} *pan*^{1} 大班)
Rich or important person. *Taipanada* the class or category to which a **taipán** belongs.

Tai-siu [tại’siu] *n* (<*C. tai*^{6} *siu*^{2} 大小)
Gambling game also called <big and small>.

Talú [tą’lu] *n*
Traditional Macanese game.

Tamarinho [tama’riɲo] **tambrinho** [tam’briɲo] *n*
Tamarind (*Tamarindus indica*).

Tambâ [tam’bạ] *vt*
1. To patch. *Tambâ calça* to patch trousers.
2. To cover, fill in. *Tambâ buraco di rua* to fill in the hole in the street.
❖***Tambâ-tacho*** [tam’bạ ‘tąču] to invite somebody at the last

minute. *Chomâ iou vai tambâ-tacho? Nádi!* Invite me to fill in for somebody who can't go? No way!

Tampípi [tam'pipi] *n*
Suitcase made of rattan or cane, often used formerly.

Tamêm [tạ'mẹŋ] *conj*
Also.

Tancá [taŋ'kạ] *n*
Small Chinese rowing boat, normally with no canvas cover.
Tancarêro [tanka'rẹro] person who lives or works of a tancá.

Tánqui ['tạŋki] *n*
1. Tank.
2. Aquarium. *Tánqui inchido di pêsse-dorado* goldfish tank or bowl.

Tánto ['tạntu] *quant*
1. An indeterminate quantity.
2. Much. *Tánto-tánto* so much.

Táp [tạp] *n* (<*C. tap*^{3} *榻*)
Toilet. *Já cai na táp* it fell down the toilet.

Tapilu [tapi'lu] *n* (<*C. ta*^{2} *pin*^{1} *lou*^{4} *打邊爐*)
Meal in which the food is brought to the table raw and then boiled in a communal pot on a special burner.

Tasquinhâ [tạski'ɲạ] *vt*
1. To steal, extract.
2. To pilfer. *syn* **Tacanâ**.

Tâu [tạw], **tâu-tâu** [tạw'tạw] *n*
Penis.

Taufú [tạw'fu], **tafú** [tạ'fu] *n* (<*C. tao*^{2} *fu*^{2} *豆腐*)
Tofu, often used in Chinese cuisine and sold in various forms.
Taufufá [tawfu'fạ] (<*C. tao*^{2} *fu*^{2} *fa*^{1} *豆腐花*) **taufú** cold tofu served with a syrup made of rock sugar (**sucre-pedra**) and ginger.

Tau-lêng [tạu'lẹŋ] *n* (<*C. tao*^{2} *ling*^{2} 斗零)
Chinese term for a five-avo coin (worth a twentieth of a pataca).

Taunái [tąw'nąi] *n* (<*C. tau*^{6} *nai*^{5} 豆奶)
Soy bean milk.

Taunâi [tąw'nąi] *adj* (<*C. tau*^{6} *lâi*^{4} 豆泥)
Worthless, despicable.
See also **Rafêro**.

Tâu-tâu [tąw'tąw] See **Tâu**.

Téfi-téfi [tęfi'tęfi] *vi adj*
1. To be afraid.
2. Shaky, due to fear.

Tel [tęl] *n*
Tael. Chinese weight. 16 taels make a catty.

Telado [te'lądu] *n*
Roof.

Têm [tęŋ] *vt*
1. To have, possess. *Iou têm dôs gato marilo* I have two tawny cats. *Vôs têm quanto filo-filo?* How many children do you have?
2. There is/are. *Têm tánto lorcha na mar* there are so many boats out at sea. *Têm pâm dóci, têm pâm salgado* there is sweet bread and savoury bread.
3. To be. *Iou têm na casa* estou em casa. *Úndi têm vôsso mai?* where is your mother?

Têmpra ['tempṛa] *n*
Condiment or collection of condiments.

Tentâ [ten'tạ] *vt*
1. To see.
2. To look. To stare at somebody or something.

Tentaçám [tenta'saŋ] *n*
Temptation. Acung'a tentaçám di Marichai that devil Marichai.

Teng-teng-lou [tẹŋ tẹŋ lọu] *n* (*<C. teng*[1] *teng*[1] *lou*[2] *叮叮佬*)
Scrap iron dealer working from door to door, who carries a rod over his shoulder with a basket hanging from each end. The *teng-teng-lou* announces his arrival by clanging a metal plate held in his hand, making a <teng...teng...> noise as he walks and thus giving rise to his name.

Terno [‘tẹrnọ] *n*
1. Shelf or board placed inside a sideboard, cupboard or bookcase.
2. Men’s suit, consisting of jacket, trousers and waistcoat.

Teto [‘tetu] *n*
Ceiling.

Tiâm [ti’ạŋ] *n* (*<C. teang*[2] *艇*)
Small, light Chinese rowing boat.

Tifim [ti’fiŋ] *n* (*<Eng. tiffin*)
1. Luncheon.
2. Snack.

Tifinâ [tifi’nạ] *n*
To lunch. *Beto logo buscâ iou vai tifinâ* Beto is going to come for me at lunchtime. *Tifinâ na oficina* to have lunch at one’s desk.

Timbil [tim’bil] *n*
Stye (in the eye).

Tim-tim pa tim-tim [tiŋ’tiŋ pa tiŋ’tiŋ] *loc adv*
Just right. With every detail correct. *Já contâ tudo tim-tim pa tim-tim,* he counted everything down to the last detail.

Tinhosa [ti’ɲọsa] *adj*
Used to describe an impertinent, sickly child.

Tipâ¹ [ti’pạ] *vt* (*<Eng. to type*)
To type.

Tipâ² [ti’pạ] *vt* (*<Eng. to tip*)
To give a tip.

Tirâ [ti'rạ] *vt*

1. To pull.
Tirâ vento [ti'rạ 'vẹntu] to clear wind with medicine. ***Tirâ-pêdo*** [ti'ra 'pẹdu], ***tirâ-pum*** [ti'rạ puŋ] to expel body gas.
2. To shoot.

Tiriçado [tiri'sądu] *adj*

Very thin, lean.

Tiro-grándi [tirǫ 'grandi] *n*

Important person (literal translation of the English <big shot>).

Títi ['titi] *n*

Aunt. *Títi-títi* aunts. *Títi-dinha* aunt who is also a god-mother. *Títi Chai* Aunt Chai.

Ti-tí[1] [ti'ti] *n*

Clamour, wilfulness. *Fazê ti-tí* to insist. *Batê ti-tí* to stamp one's feet and make a noise in order to drive home a point.

Ti-tí[2] [ti'ti] *vt*

To bang one object with another. *Tí-ti prato co colê* to bang a spoon on a plate.

Tiz [tis] *quant*

A small portion. *Comê ung'a tiz di aroz* to eat just a drop of rice.

Tocâ [tǫ'kạ] *vt*

1. To touch.
2. To gamble and win, guess the lottery.

Tóc-tóc [tǫk'tǫk] *adj*

Crazed, beveled.

Tôm-tôm [tǫŋ'tǫŋ] *n*

1. Piece of candy wrapped in paper.
2. Dried animal excrement, especially from a dog or a cat.
3. Pejorative name for Macanese descendants living in Hong Kong. See **Macau-Paio**.

Tôm-tôm-môm-tôm [tọŋ'tọŋ mọŋ'tọŋ] *adj* (*<C. mong² tong²* 懵懂)
Clumsy person who always gets mixed up, dabbler,

Tópe ['tọpi] *n*
Compartment in a home, parlour, small room.

Torâ [tọ'rạ] *vt*
To toast. *Torâ pâm* to toast bread.
Torâ português [tọ'rạ portu'gẹs] used to describe a person who can speak perfect Portuguese, with an affected accent.

Tornâ [tọr'rạ] *vt*
1. To return. *Tornâ vêm* He came again.
2. Again.
3. Once more. *Tornâ chomâ iou* he called me once more.

Torto ['tọrtọ] *adj*
Twisted. *Torto-ravirado* stretched out. *Torto-torto* twisted.

Trabalo [tra'bąlọ] *n*
Hard, expensive, difficult. *Assí trabalo ganhâ* it is so hard to win. *Trabalo siviço* difficult task.

Trás [trąs] *adv*
Behind.
❖***Trás di porta*** [trąs di 'pọrta] very near. *Ano Nôvo têm na trás di porta* New Year is just around the corner.

Tratamento [trata'mẹntu] *n*
1. Treatment.
2. Get-together, social life. *Nôm têm tratamento* he doesn't have a social life.

Trelâ [trẹ'lạ] *vi*
1. To talk. *Vêm-câ trelâ unchinho* come a chat a little.
2. To chatter.

Trepâ [trẹ'pạ] *vt*
1. To climb, go up. *Trepâ cama* to go up to bed.
Trepâ caréta to get on the bus.

Trepâ telado to climb onto the roof.
2. To become drunk after imbibing alcohol.

Tréta [ʻtrẹta] *n*
Dodge, idle talk, rigmarole. *Sâm tudo tréta* it's all a sham.

Tricada [tri'kada] *n*
Leap, throw. *Dâ ung'a tricada pa águ* to jump into the water. *Dâ ung'a tricada na águ* to dive in.

Triol [tri'ọl] *n*
Marble (glass ball).

Tudo-óra [tu'dọra] *adv*
Always, any time, at any moment.

Tudúm [tu'duŋ] *n*
Broad-brimmed Chinese hat made of **óla** or cane with a rattan brim. A **tudúm** is worn in either sun or rain.

Tuna [ʻtuna] *n*
Tuna.
Tuna di musiquêro [ʻtuna di muzi'kẹro] gathering of strong musicians who would dress up at Carnival and go out to play in the streets, and at parties.

Turum [tu'ruŋ] *n*
Traditional Macanese game.

Tu-tum-piám [tu tum pi'aŋ] *n*
(<*C. tou[4] tong[3] peng[2] 頭痛病*)
Nincompoop, usually an older person of no worth.

Ucho [‘učo] *n* (<*P. Um* + *M. cium*)
Kiss. *Já vêm co ung'a ucho* he/she came proffering a kiss. *Atúto qui boniteza, ja dâ ung'a ucho pa su mai* sweet Atútu kissed his mother.

Ufa! [‘ufa] *interj*
Expression of fear or relief.

Ui-di [‘widi] *quant*
A lot, very. *Comizaina ui-di saboroso* very tasty food .
Ui-di sim! [‘widi siŋ] very good!

Umbigo [um'bigu], **imbigo** [im'bigu] *n*
Navel.
❖ ***Umbigo-pegado*** [um'bigu pe'gądu], ***umbigo-chapado*** [um'bigu ča'pądu] used to describe people who are inseparable, hand in glove.

Umpôco [uŋ'pọko] See **Unchinho**.

Uncento [un'sentu] *quant*
1. One hundred. *Uncento fora* a hundred-odd.
2. Many. *Tâ papiâ uncento di parabiça* he/she is talking nonsense.

Unchinho [uɲ'čiɲu] *quant*
Very little. *Já faltâ unchinho* there was hardly any left. *Iou querê unchinho na-más* I just want a tiny bit. *Unchinho-unchinho ora* from time to time.

Unçôm [un'sọŋ] See **Onçóm**.

Úndi [‘undi] *adv*
Where. *Úndi já vai?* where did you/he/she go? *Vôs têm na úndi?* where are you? *Úndi vôs tâ vai?* where are you going? *Úndi lôgo têm?* where can it be? where will there be any? *Nós sabê sâm úndi* we know where it is.

Unsóm [un'sọŋ] See **Onçóm**.

Ung'a ['uŋa] *núm, det & det pro*
One. *Ung'a namás* only one. *Ung'a semana ung'a vez* once a week. *Ung'a hómi co ung'a mulé* a man and a woman.

Ungsóm [uŋ'sọŋ] See **Onçóm**.

Upâ [u'pạ] *vt*
1. To hit, beat somebody up, whack. *Upâ di bêm-fêto* to give a good hiding.
2. To smack a child's behind.

Usâ [u'zạ] *vt*
1. To employ, use, utilize.
2. To wear. *Usâ rópa* to put on clothing. *Usâ bôbo* to dress up.
3. To put on shoes. *Usâ sapato nôvo* to wear new shoes.

Uví [u'vi] *vt*
To listen, hear. *Iou uví falâ* I heard.
Uví! listen! *Úndi vôs já uví?* where did you hear [that]? *J'uví?* did you hear?

Vaca [ʻvạka] *n*

1. Cow.
2. Beef. *Vaca chacháu margoso* Macanese dish of stewed beef with bitter melon. ***Vaca mínchi*** [ʻvạka ʻmiɲči] minced beef.
3. Corpulent woman. *Ung'a nhônha bem di vaca* a very large lady. *Ela assí vaca* she is built like the back of a bus.

Vacoco [va'kọko] *adj*

Large, corpulent. *Ui-di vacoco!* so big!

Vagar [va'gạr] *adv & n*

1. Slowly, leisurely. *Vagar-vagar* very slowly. *Vagar subí* to go up slowly. *Vagar-vagar andâ* walk slowly!
2. Time, free time, opportunity. *Iou nôm têm vagar* I don't have time. *Si têm vagar lôgo vêm* I'll come if I have time.

Vai [vại] *vi*

To go.

Vai … vêm sentence structure used to indicate a repeated action or thought. *Andâ vai andâ vêm* to go from one place to another. *Corê vai corê vêm* to run around. *Falâ vai falâ vêm* to say and to say again.

Valéta [va'lẹta] *n*

Drainpipe, drain.

Vánda [ʻvạnda] *n*

Side. *Pa estung'a vánda* round here.

Vánda di trás [ʻvạnda di trạs] rear part, behind.

Alí-vánda [ali 'vạnda] beyond.

Vangueâ [vạŋgi'ạ] *vi* (<*C. wan*^{4} 暈)

1. To feel faint, feel dizzy.
2. To faint.

Vangueado [vạŋgi'ạdu] *adj*

Giddy, dizzy.

Vantú [van'tu] *adj* (<*M. bantut*)

Jinxed, riled. Condition of a

person, cake or other food once it has been affected by the evil eye or ill winds. *Siara já intrâ, iou sua bôlo já ficâ vantú* the lady came in and my cake was ruined.

bariga vantú [ba'riga van'tu] stomach upset.

Varê [vą'rẹ] *vt*

To sweep.

❖ ***Varê rua*** [vą'rẹ 'rua] to wander around, always be out.

Vasculiâ [vąskuli'ạ] *vt*

To snoop, investigate, search.

Vassóra [va'sǫra] *n*

Broom, brush.

Vassôra pena [va'sǫra 'pęna] feather duster with rattan handle.

Vassôra bambú [va'sǫra bam'bu] stiff broom made from vime or bamboo strips for sweeping earth or wet surfaces.

Vassôra côco [va'sǫra 'kọko] brush made from coconut fibre used to sweep indoors.

Vazâ [vą'za] *vt*

1. To fill, serve. *Vazâ chá* to pour a cup of tea.
2. To run. *Telado vazâ água* the water is running off the roof.

Vazo-fula ['vąsu 'fula] *n*

Vase.

Vê [vẹ] *vt*

1. To look.
2. To see.
3. To seem, look like.

Veado [vi'ądu] *adj*

Cuckold.

Vedade [vẹ'dąde] *n*

Truth.

Vegónha [vẹ'gǫṇa] *n*

Shame. *Iou vegónha* I'm ashamed. *Qui vegónha!* what a shame! *Nancassá vegónha, da mostrâ* don't be shy, show us.

Véla[1] ['vęla] *n*

Candle. *Pegâ véla companhâ*

procissám to take part in a candelit procession.

Véla[2] [‘vęla] *adj e n*

Old woman. *Véla-véla* old women.

Vêlo [‘vęlọ] *adj & n m*

Old man. *Vêlo-vêlo* old men. *Nhum vêlo* an elderly man. ❖ ***Macaco vêlo*** [ma’kaku ‘vęlọ] (i) astute person; (ii) rogue.

Vêlo-công [vęlọ’koŋ] *n*

Old man.

Vêm [vęŋ] *vi*

To come. *Vêm câ!* come here! *Já vêm?* has he/she come? *Ilôtro nádi vêm* they’re not coming. *Fazê iou vêm pa qui cuza?* why did you ask me to come?

Vento [‘vęntu] *n*

1. Wind.
2. Air, gas.
3. Breath, respiration.

Vento marado [‘vęntu ma’rądu] laboured breathing.

4. Ill wind, stuffy.

Viazâ [vią’za] *vi*

To travel.

Viázi [vi’ązi] *n*

Journey.

Vida-fêde [‘vida ’fęde] *adj*

Annoying, tedious. *Qui vida-fêde!* How annoying!

Vilám [vi’laŋ] *n*

Villain.

Génio di vilám [‘ǯeniu di vi’laŋ] bad-tempered, always wanting the upper hand.

Vinho ladrám [‘viɲọ la’draŋ] *n*

Chinese medicine consisting of herbs preserved in a highly alcoholic Chinese wine.

Virâ [vi’rạ] *vt*

1. To turn, direct.

Virâ ôlo [vi'rạ 'ọlu] to roll one's eyes in despair.

❖ ***Virâ mám*** [vi'ra maŋ] in the flash of an eye, in an instant.

❖ ***Virâ beço*** [vi'ra 'bẹsu] to talk, chat.

2. To return. *Iou virâ respondê* I answered again.

❖ ***Virâ cacús*** [vi'rạ kạ'kus] to cause trouble, problems.

Virâ ficâ [vi'rạ fi'kạ] to change into, be converted.

❖ ***Virâ tap*** [vi'rạ tạp] *syn* ***Virâ cacús***.

❖ ***Virâ-virâ vêm*** [vi'rạ vi'rạ vẹŋ] come in sometime, come when you can.

Visaga [vi'zạga] *n*

Hinge.

Volontrôm [vọlọn'trọŋ], **bolontrôm** [bọlọn'trọŋ]

Fat, clumsy person.

Vong-pit [vọŋ'pit] *n* (<*C. wong*[4] *pei*[2] *黃皮*)

Wampee (*Clausena lansium*), Chinese fruit the size of a grape with a brown/yellow skin and white pulp.

Vulto ['vultọ] *n*

1. Body.

2. Indistinct shape.

Vun [vun] *n* (<*C. wun*[2] *碗*)

Ceramic bowl. *Já comê dôs vun di arôz agora querê más* he/she ate two bowls of rice and still wants more.

Xale ['čąli] See **chale**.

Xerâ ['čẹ'rạ] See **Cherâ**.

Xicra ['čikra] *n*

Cup, teacup. *Dâ ung'a xicra di chá pa iou* bring me a cup of tea.

Xirí [či'ri] See **Chiri**.

Xiripo [či'ripu] See **chiripo**.

Zaprecê [zapre'sẹ] *vi*
To disappear. *Azinha zaprecê di iou-sua diante!* get out of my sight!

Zaragata [zara'gata] *n*
Tumult, hubbub.

Zaragatéra [zaga'tẹra] *n*
Hooligan.

Zavanâ [zava'nạ] *vt*
To shake.

Zinguâ [ziŋ'gwạ] *vt*
1. To scull (a boat).
2. To hit.
3. To harness.

Zuní [zu'ni] *vi*
To buzz, drone. *Pegâ apito zuní* to blow a whistle.

Zunidela [zuni'dela] *n*
Buzz, hum. *Zunidela di bicho-mel* humming of bees.

APPENDIX: MACANESE NAMES

The wealth of Maquista is not only limited to words and idioms; relationships and social context, life experiences and a shared past have led to unusual forms of address in the tiny city of Macao. One aspect of this is the names by which people are known. This Appendix is divided into three categories of names, with different social functions.

The first category is formal Christian names, registered in birth, baptismal or other official records. Arquiticlínio, Eustrógia, Hotildes, Marmétrio, Onófre, Prosdócimo, Saxeferato, Trôpos, all reflect the profoundly Catholic nature of Macanese society during a more conservative, inward-looking period when traditions were closely followed.

The second group consists of family or pet names (more commonly referred to as *nómi-di-casa, nómi-dóci* or *nómi di família* in Macao) such as Ato, Adé, Api, Bebé, Bichim, Calinho, Chai-Chai, Chencho, Dado, Gegé, Janjám, Mica, Peca, Púchi. These names were used affectionately in close social circles, especially the family. In most cases, it was the Chinese amah, with at best a very rudimentary understanding of Portuguese, who would give this name to the child in her care.

Finally, there is a selection of nicknames. It is a commonplace, if somewhat exaggerated, that the Macanese are known by their nicknames. Thus each person, with his or her idiosyncrasies, is truly identified and given an individual label which, ironically, also conveys a sense of belonging to the community, for better or for worse. Nicknames can range from Cemitério Vong-Hin ["Vong-Hin Cemetery"], the brothers Duro-duro e Móli-Móli ["Hardy-Hardy" and "Limpy-Limpy"], Esqueleto ["Skeleton"], Maria-Já-Se-Vê ["Maria Let's See"], Pêndulo ["Pendulum"], Quarenta-Seis ["Forty-Six"] nicknames that portray the Macanese sense of humour, malice, and sharp social observations of everything and everyone.

For obvious reasons, all the names included in this section are intended for the record, rather than to identify specific people. There has been no intention to target any particular person; rather, to pay homage to that simple yet complex figure: the *maquista chapado.*

1. Unusual Christian names

Abundância
Adalberto
Adalrico
Adeodato
Adroaldo
Áfra
Agapito
Agripina
Albérico
Aldegundes
Aldevina
Alípio
Alménia
Almídia
Amabília
Amandina
Anália
Ananias
Anardo
Andrónico
Anfitrite
Aprígio
Aquilânia
Argemiro
Argentina
Armantina
Arquibaldo
Arquitriclínio
Artimídoro
Artimísia
Astéria
Ataúlfo
Aulisa
Auriza
Balbina
Basilida
Beanina
Belgina
Beliza
Belizário
Beltra
Bemvinda
Benício(a)
Bertolina
Blandina
Bomfilho
Bórgia
Borromeu
Bráulia
Brazildo
Brício
Cacilda
Câncio
Cantídio
Canuta
Capitolina
Capristano
Carciano
Carmelinda
Carmelito

Cassiano
Catalina
Catulínio
Celanira
Celorino
Cerial
Cezarião
Cinfrónia
Circulina
Ciríaco
Cirilo
Clariza
Clélio
Clodomiro
Clodulfo
Clorina
Corfilha
Corfira
Coriolano
Corsina
Crescência(o)
Cresmilda
Crisanto
Crismila
Crispim
Crispiniano
Cundegundes
Cupertino
Damasceno
Daurísia
Délcia
Delcimina
Demetrino
Demisina
Dermelinda
Dermina
Desidério
Despondoleur
Dídimo
Dinamérica
Dombelo
Domiciano
Domicília
Domitília
Domnolo
Dorindo
Drusila
Dulcelino
Dulcino
Edelberto
Edeltrudes
Edriz
Elcrida
Eleazar
Elesina
Eleutério
Eliseu
Elizário
Elnora
Elóia
Elvídio
Emerenciana

Emérico
Emérita
Emiliana
Engrácia
Epifânia
Epigménio
Ercília
Ercina
Ermídio
Ermila
Ermina
Erondina
Esméria
Esnaida
Esperidião
Estelca
Esténio
Esterbino
Estilito
Etelberto
Etelmira
Etelvira
Eudóxia
Eufrásia
Eufrónia
Eufrosina
Euquério
Euquíria
Eusígnio
Eustáquio
Eustrógia
Eusvergílio
Euvegilda
Evândole
Everdina
Ezilda
Favorino
Felisbino
Filinto
Filoteia
Firminiano
Flória
Floriberto
Floriza
Fortino
Frutuoso
Fulgêncio
Galvino
Gaudêncio
Gaudioso
Geovanina
Geralberto
Glafira
Glicéria
Goares
Guardiato
Gumesindo
Gúrtio
Heliodoro
Hermância
Hermerina
Hermilo

Hermipo
Hermócrates
Hildalinda
Hildebrando
Himócrates
Hipátia
Honorina
Horto
Hotildes
Ildefonso
Ildegarde
Iluminada
Inésia
Ionel
Iraida
Irénio(a)
Isalina
Isilda
Ismália
Isménia
Ivásio
Jesuína
Jorgínia
Josino(a)
Julina
Julita
Laertes
Laurência
Lavínia
Lealmidas
Lenilda
Leocádio(a)
Leona
Leôncio
Leoneltina
Leonídea
Leonílio
Leonisa
Leontina
Leovigildo(a)
Levínia
Libânio
Líbia
Libório
Licénio
Licínio
Lidina
Lidivina
Lindamira
Lindoro
Lizaura
Ludovina(o)
Lusolinda
Mâncio(a)
Marmétrio
Maurílio
Meinardo
Mejelina
Melânia
Melcíades
Melécio
Melentina

Melquíades
Metrodora
Milentina
Míltia
Milvínia
Minervino
Nazário
Nepomuceno
Nicásio
Nicéforo
Numa
Olderico
Onófre
Osmia
Osmínia
Otília
Paciência
Pamfílio
Pancrácio
Parísia
Parménio
Pascásio
Pascoela
Patrocínio
Paulico
Pelágia
Perpétuo
Petrona
Petronila
Plácida
Plínio
Pompílio
Porcida
Possidónio
Príamo
Prisco
Procópio
Próculo
Prosdócimo
Prudêncio
Prudente
Pulquéria
Pulquíria
Querubina
Quintéra
Quirino
Quitéria(o)
Ramildo
Régis
Remegino
Remígio
Renovato
Revogata
Rigoberto
Rosaloína
Rosaura
Rubina
Rubye
Saladino
Satiro
Satúrio
Saturnino(a)

Saxeferato
Secundino
Sedaliza
Segisfredo
Selidónio
Selmira
Selónio
Séptimo
Seráfia
Seralina
Serrapiana
Sidérico
Sigismundo
Simiana
Simôa
Simplício(a)
Sinibaldo
Sulpícia
Teclo
Temiro
Tenório
Teobaldo
Teodolina
Teotónio
Terêncio
Terezina
Tibúrcio
Tílio
Tolentino
Tomásia
Toríbio
Torquato
Tranquilino
Trôpos
Túlia(o)
Ubaldino
Ubaldo
Udília
Uladislau
Ulina
Ulrica
Umbelina
Urbina
Ursina
Ursulina
Vassalo
Vérico
Veridiana
Vicência
Violante
Vitaliano
Voltaire
Xisto
Zaida
Zelina
Zelindo(o)
Zelindra
Zilhão
Zocé
Zófimo
Zorina

2. Family ames

A-Béu
Acaio
À-Chai
Àchico
Acho
Achuce
Achúcho
Adé
Ading
Ado
A-Fét
À-Fí
A-Fú
Ajú
Alica
Alichai
Alíchi
Aling
A-Lú
Aneng
Anica
Anina
Aninha
Á-Nu
A-Pái
A-Pâi
A-Pi
A-Tí
A-Tó
Ato
Atúto
Bachai
Béba
Bebé
Béca
Bécas
Béni
Ber
Béti
Betita
Beto
Bibico
Bicho
Bita
Bítchi or Bítchim
Bútchi
Caco
Calim
Calinho
Calito
Calo
Caló
Calóssi
Ch'ông-Ch'ông
Châi-Châi
Chaine
Charly
Chencho

Chente
Cheubi
Chicha
Chichi
Chichita
Chicho
Chichóni
Chinto
Chiquito
Chiu-chiu
Chúcho
Cóque
Cuca
Dado
Delfe
Dête
Dico
Didi
Dídi
Dim-dim
Doobee
Dudú
Dúdu
Édi
Édo
Éto
Fáti
Fi
Filinha
Filó
Fina-chai

Fó-Fio
Frédi
Fredo
Gabi
Gêge
Gegé (Jejé)
Geio (Jeio)
Géni
Geninha
Giga
Gigi
Gígui
Gija
Giraffe
Gito
Gugo
Gúsing
Guta
Guto
Icha
Ichi
Ico
Inha
Ito
Janjám
Jéca
Jéri
Jóni
Jozico
Jujú
Júni

Júni-Boy
Láli
Lalo
Lano
Lélé
Lélo
Licas
Lilit
Lilito
Lita
Lito
Litos
Lóli
Lúdi
Lulú
Manachai
Manecas
Mano
Manú
Mariazinha
Marica
Marichai
Maricú
Ména
Mica
Mico
Miguelim
Miguelito
Mimí
Mími
Mimita
Mina
Miro
Mui-mui
Naio
Naldo
Nandinha
Nando
Nano
Narí
Néca
Néco
Néné
Néni
Nêta
Néti
Néu-néu
Nico
Nina
Ninho
Nini
Ninito
Nino
Ninótchka
Nita
Nito
Nôi-Nôi
Nónó
Óli
Paco
Panchito
Peca

Pedrico
Pedrito
Picarú
Pipa
Piu-piu
Pom-pom
Púchi
Puchito
Quitinha
Régi
René
Rique
Ri-Rí
Róge
Sonny
Sussú
Taco
Táncho
Tato
Telé
Tereng
Téri
Tété
Tico
Tico-Tico
Tim-tim
Tininha
Tóne
Toneca
Tonico
Tonim
Toninho
Tony
Tótó
Vaca
Zeca
Zequinhas
Zete
Zézé
Zinha
Zinho
Zito

3. Nicknames[1]

Abibe
Abissínio
Abú[2]
À-Ch'á
A-Chát
Acho-Bolacho
Achúchi
A-Ki-Ki
Á-Kó-Pê-Fêde[3]
Alan-Delon
Alau
Al-Di-La[4]
Alemão
Ali-babá
Alipám
Almirante-Lodo
A-Mó
A-Mong
Ana Boonaga
Anão
Angelão
Antigonço
Apacho
Apa-fêde
A-Pái-Sâm (fam.)
Apan-Có
A-Pâng
Apinha
Áp-Keok[5]
Áp-Keok-Pau
A-Tâi
Atão
Ateu
Atú-Chong
À-Ú
A-Ui
Avô
Avó Iói Iã
Babú
Banana
Batata
Bazuka
Beata[6]

[1] The English names provided in the footnotes are a literal translation of the original nicknames. They have been included with the sole purpose of giving the reader a better understanding of the original flavour and meaning.

[2] "*Grandfather*".

[3] "*The eldest brother with smelly feet*".

[4] Who was very fond of a song with this title that was popular in the late 1950s.

[5] "*Duck feet*", describing how his feet looked when he walked.

[6] "*Fag-End*", who smoked cigarettes down to the very last drag.

Bebé-Branco
Bebé-Gordo
Bebé-Preto
Bébé-Rato
Bécho
Béri-béri
Betita
Bexigoso-em-dois-segundos
Bi or Bi-Bosco or Bôsca
Bita-Cacâi
Boca-Fêde
Bocage
Bôi
Boi-Apis
Bolo-Bolo
Bombordo-estibordo[7]
Bon-Beuf
Boneca
Branca-de-Neve
Bucha
Caça-Minas
Cacatua
Café
Cai-Cai
Calito-T'âu-Kai[8]

[7] "*Larboard-Starboard* ", a woman whose buttocks were heavy enough to make her body swing from side to side when walking.
[8] "*Calito, the chicken thief* ".

Calito-Maluco
Canivete
Capão
Capela
Capí-Chai[9]
Capigalo
Cára-de-aço[10]
Carambola
Carapau
Caréca-Letrado[11]
Cascais
Catamonte or Carta-Monte[12]
Câu-Sât
Cemitério-Vóng-Hin[13]
Ch'ât T'ong or Hông Ch'ât
Ch'ât-Sâi
Ch'ông-Mei-Mei
Ch'ôn-Tói-Azul

[9] "*Little Capí*", brother of "Tai Capí" ("*Big Capí*").
[10] "*Steely Face*", who wouldn't smile under any circumstances.
[11] "*Bald-Lawyer*".
[12] "*Carry-the-mountain* ", a direct translation into Maquista of "Toi San", the Cantonese name for Tamagnini Barbosa District, in the northern part of Macao.
[13] Who used to go to the cemetery to collect "vong hin", a maggot that he used as fishing bait.

Chácha
Chainito
ChangKeng-Meng
Cháng-Páu
Chá-Siu
Châu-Ké
Chéca
Chéna
Chia
Chí-chi
Chichi-Pái
Chico-Aflito
Chico-Bate-Pé
Chico-Chai
Chico-Direi [14]
Chico-Fán-Chiu
Chico-Fi-Sen
Chicóia
Chico-Lao-Sung
Chicolât
Chico-Madame
Chico-Maluco[15]
Chico-Mama[16]

[14] "*Chico-how-should-I-put it*", who started almost every sentence with "Como direi…" ("How should I put it").
[15] "*Crazy-Chico*".
[16] "*Chico-Breast*", brother of "Chico-Teta" ("*Chico-Tit*").

Chico-Mano[17]
Chico-Menina[18]
Chico-Mente[19]
Chico-Micróbio[20]
Chico-Pangalhadas
Chico-Pari-Rato
Chico-Pêlo-Pé
Chico-Pé-Pesado
Chico-Preto
Chico-Rapariga
Chico-Tau Nai
Chico-Tau-Tau
Chico-Teta[21]
Chíli-Ponta-Céu
Chincha
Chinguiço
Chinto
Chiquitim
Chirit

[17] "*Big-Brother-Chico*".
[18] "*Chico-Little-Girl*".
[19] "*Chico-ly*", who, whenever possible, would exhaustively, tirelessly and abusively, make use of adverbs.
[20] "*Chico-Microbe*", who was obsessed with the wild idea that everywhere is infested with viruses and bacteria.
[21] "*Chico-Tit*", brother of "Chico-Mama" ("*Chico-Breast*").

Chivit
Chorão
Chou-Fú
Chü-Chai or Pequenetótis
Chúchu
Chupa-Dêdo[22]
Cindarella-Stepsister[23]
Conchita
Coxo
Crocodilo
Cú-de-Chumbo
Cú-de-Pato
Dairy Farm
Dee Jay
Dête Tau-Tau
Dica
Doutor-Rosca
Duro-Duro[24]
Esqueleto
Estica
Fán-fán
Fantasma
Fantochêro
Farelo
Faruk
Fei-Chü
Fei-Tut
Ferro-o-bico
Fó-Ché-Tau
Gafanhoto
Garrafám
General
Goio
Gong-Gong
Gozo-Bébé
Hác-Kuai-Chai
Half-Man[25]
Hám I Pó[26]
Iam Chi Ku
Ieong-Ch'ung-T'au
Ieong-Mé-Si
Ito Cacai
Jacaré
Jambulám
James-Dean
Jap
Japonês

[22] "*Thumb-Sucker*", who carried on this habit until he was nineteen years old.

[23] Who was ugly in comparison with her sister, just like the stepsister in the popular fairytale.

[24] "*Hardy-hardy*", brother of Móle-Móle ("*Limpy-limpy*").

[25] Who was in fact a hairy woman.

[26] "*Salted-Fish-Madam*", who earned the nickname due to her intense and somewhat unbearable perspiration.

Jo-achim
João-Faz-Fato[27]
João-Môco
José Conde
José-Carta-Sôm
José-Chiripo
José-dos-Bigodes[28]
José-Taludo
Kâi-Chông[29]
Kâi-Kâi
Kâi-P'ou
Kilo
King-Kong
Lalau
Lât Fú
Lat-T'át-Fei
Lausim
Leng-Tong-Kuang (fam.)
Língua-de-Ferro[30]
Litro
Lobumba

[27] "*João, the suit maker*", a Chinese tailor, well known in the Portuguese community.
[28] "*Moustache-José*", who was very proud of his bushy moustache.
[29] "*Chicken-Bug*" in Cantonese, who was a great fan of prostitutes (referred to locally as "chicken").
[30] "*Iron-Tongue*", who was renowned for his exceptional skills as a lover.

Ló-Pak
Lou-Fu-Chai
Luz-Tou-Niu
Macaco
Macaco-velho
Má-Chai-Siqueira
Maco
Madame Machado[31]
Madre
Ma-Mio-Ngán
Mamute[32]
Manetas (fam.)
Manête
Manga
Mano Mono
Maria Azul
Maria Trelé
Maria-Acheng
Maria-Já-Se-Vê[33]
Maria-Roda-Baixo
Maria-Tranca
Mari-Rato
Mar-Picado
Máu-Cristão
Mau-Si-Kón or Mau-Kón

[31] She was a very popular teacher of French.
[32] "*Mammoth*", who was extremely hairy.
[33] "*Maria-Let's-See*", who would never give a prompt answer to any question.

Máu-Vong
Max
Mendonçada (fam.)
Meno-Niu-Pun
Mínchi
Ministro
Min-Pau
Moca
Môcho
Móli-Móli[34]
Môlo
Monkey-Roza
Monteiro-das-Barbas
Mordaça
Mou-Chák-Tong[35]
Mou-Si-Fât[36]
Mugica or Mujica
Mula
Nerú
Ngau-Pin
Nhé-nhé
Nina-Fêde
Nolascada (fam.)
Olho-de-boi

[34] "*Limpy-limpy*", brother of Duro-Duro ("*Hardy-hardy*").
[35] "*Mao-Tse-Tung*", who resembled the old Chairman.
[36] "*No-Bum*".

Olimpopot
One-eyed-Jack
Ôvo-Estrelado
Padeiro
Padre
Padre-Tareco
Pai-de-boi[37]
Pak-Kuai
Palito
Pancraciada (fam.)
Papa-Charruto[38]
Papaia
Paquita
Parado-Corido
Pát Chau I[39]
Pau-Pau
Pau-Preto
Pé-de-Bambu
Pedro-Mé-Mé
Pê-Grosso[40]
Peixe

[37] "*Ox-Daddy*", who herded the oxen that carried the drinking water to the old Conde S. Januário Hospital, when there was a water shortage.
[38] "*Cigar-Eater*", who used to dress like a man and has a passion for cigars.
[39] "*Octupus*" in Cantonese.
[40] "*Thick-Foot*"

Pêndulo[41]
Penico-de-ouro
Pequenái
Pequinitátis
Perú-Depenado
Pi-chop[42]
Pinéu
Pinky
Pinóia
Pintoca
Piolho
Pisco
Pivête
Põe-te-a-pau
Pôpo (fam.)
Preto
Quarenta-seis[43]
Quéu-quéu
Radar[44]
Rosalhada (fam.)
Rui-Tôrto
Russo (Ruço)
Sábu
Sai-Kó-Zéze
Saltia
Samari
Sán-Chá
San-Keng-Lok
Santé
Shit-Man[45]
Si-T'ap-Kói
Só-P'au
Só-Pí
Sousa-Barbeiro
Sousa-Corneta
Sousa-Maneta
Superman
T'in-Kâi
T'ou-Chai
Tabléu[46]
Tai-Capí[47]
Tái-Ch'ak

[41] "*Pendulum*", who used to rock his body from side to side when walking, just as the nickname suggests.
[42] An employee of the old Macao Lyceum, whose job it was to record teachers' absences by putting a chop in the register.
[43] "*Forty-Six*", which was, according to gossip, her bust measurement.
[44] Just like the nickname's original meaning, he picked up everything, from a distance and even in advance.
[45] Who had the extremely bad luck of stopping his motorbike just above a sewer when it burst.
[46] Who was known to pronounce the French word "tableau" in the Portuguese way.
[47] See *Capí-Chai.*

Tái-Ko-Zéze[48]
Tai-hin-Ngau
Tai-Min-Pau
Tai-Nin-P'ó[49]
Tai-Só
Tá-Lán-Tin-Wá[50]
Tancachói (fam.)
Tancareiro
Tan-Tan
Táp-Siac Sisters
Tarrique
Tartaruga
Tarzan
Tau-Fu-Kok
Tau-Nén
Têta-Chai[51]
Tico-Tico
Tilipum
Tin Kâi
Tira Pum[52]
Tirita
Tôio
Tôn Tôn
Tórta
Tótó
Toura
Treme-treme[53]
Tufám
Very-Good-Chipido (fam.)[54]
Vong-Chau
Whiskey
Zeca-Coxo
Zé-China
Zé-Nove-Nomes
Zé-Taludo
Zito Maluco

[48] "*Big-Zeze*". Although not related to Sai-ko-Zeze ("*Little-Zeze*"), these two Josés were neighbours, so they were distinguished by older (*Tai-Ko*) and younger (*Sai-Ko*).
[49] "*Big-Breasts*" in Cantonese.
[50] "*Phone-Cracker*".
[51] "*Little-Tit*", who was flat-chested.
[52] "*Fart-Shooter*", who was very proud to have fired 36 shots in a row.
[53] "*Shaky-shaky*", who shivered and trembled all over when irritated.
[54] According to one version, the nickname was originated from a comment that one of the sisters had made about a hat displayed in a boutique: "*Very good...mas un-poco chipido*" ("very nice, but it's flat though").

TITLE
Maquista Chapado. Vocabulary and Expressions in Macao's Portuguese Creole
translated from the Portuguese original:
Maquista Chapado: Vocabulário e expressões do crioulo português de Macau.
(Instituto Internacional de Macau, 2001)

AUTHORS
Miguel Senna Fernandes & Alan Norman Baxter

PUBLISHER
Cultural Institute of the Macao S.A.R. Government

TRANSLATOR
Marie Imelda MacLeod

COORDINATION
DEIP (Studies, Research and Publications Division)

ART DIRECTOR
Victor Marreiros

GRAPHIC DESIGN AND COVER
Gisela Viegas

COLOUR SEPARATION AND PRINTING
Tipografia Macau Hung Heng Ltda.

PRINT-RUN
500 copies

1ST EDITION
November 2004

ISBN 99937-0-069-X